I See Her . . .

I See Her . . .

Jerrilyn Black

Born and raised in El Paso, Texas, Jerrilyn Black is a licensed clinical social worker and psychotherapist currently residing in Washington, DC. While Jerrilyn has found healing through creative writing since childhood, *I See Her . . .,* is her first poetry collection. Jerrilyn loves all things pop culture, is at peace during walks in nature, and finds joy in a good, healthy laugh.

Copyright © 2022 Jerrilyn Black
www.jerrilynblack.com
jerriblack@gmail.com

ISBN 978-0-578-36333-2

Edited and designed by Tell Tell Poetry

Printed in the United States of America

First Printing, 2022

To Molly. I will always love you, and my heart will always miss you.

Contents

. . . in my everyday fight to be enough

. . . in the multidimensional and prismatic aspects of my faith

. . . in my reverence for all my relations

. . . in my joy, magic, strength, and possibilities

. . . in my healing

Acknowledgments

I give the utmost thanks to the Creator and my loving ancestors who led me to and through the writing of this collection, and guide, bless and protect me each day. To my mother and father, Margie and Johnny, thank you for always believing in and nurturing my potential with your wisdom, patience, humor and love. I'm also thankful for the countless friends and family members who listened to my worries and encouraged me to keep writing and visioning when I wanted to give up. Your optimism and kindnesses made all the difference. And I send abundant appreciation to the Sanctuaries DC for helping me to rediscover my creative voice, and to the editors and designers at Tell Tell Poetry for helping to bring *I See Her . . .* to life.

And THANK YOU to the over two dozen women who participated as storytellers in this project. You each sat with me for hours in my living room or across from me on a computer screen while I asked you questions about your lives. You did this with openness, vulnerability, and trust before I even knew how this collection would come into being. I'm truly humbled by your belief in me and honored that you said yes to this journey. I saw myself in your beautiful, courageous, heartbreaking, love-filled stories, and I saw you in mine. Your stories are your lives, glittering with rays of sunshine, filtering light through hurting spaces, bearing gifts of truth and healing. Your stories are you. With so much love and gratitude, thank you!

A Note to the Reader

I'm so thankful that you decided to pick up this book and open its pages. In 2017, I began what was called the *Women's Storytelling Project* where I interviewed over two dozen women about aspects of their lives. That project led to *I See Her . . .*, a collection of poems and essays inspired by their stories and experiences. This title felt so right because being seen was an overarching theme amongst the storytellers. Themes of love, pain, trauma, healing, faith, family, loss—and did I mention healing—also surfaced.

I invited the storytellers to include their names with the pieces they inspired. Some chose to appear with full names, first names, or initials, while others opted to show up anonymously. No matter how they show up, their stories and experiences are seen and welcome!

As a clinical social worker and psychotherapist, I'd be remiss if I didn't say that the storytellers have never been or will ever be treated by me. Also, none of the works in this collection are representative of anyone I have provided psychotherapy to, nor are they meant to provide clinically therapeutic advice.

With that said, my sincerest desire is that people reading this collection see themselves in it. I also hope that it broadens the collective space we give to each other to be seen, in whatever ways we choose to show up. And, as an offering to the world, I hope *I See Her . . .* leads to greater healing, joy, and magic.

With love,
Jerrilyn

I See Her . . .

I see her . . .

One day, as I was pinning up my hair in the bathroom mirror, my reflection started speaking to me.

Hello, my love. May I take you on a journey to experience the beautiful, the sad, the uplifting, the heartbreaking, the joyous, and everything in between?

My hands froze in my hair. I was completely baffled as I quietly stared at her moving lips, wondering if I was hallucinating.

She chuckled at my confusion and said with assurance, *You're in your right mind. I'm here because I want you to see.*

My eyebrows moved up and down with curiosity as I weighed walking away, jumping into bed, and starting the day again, or entertaining my reflection's request. Ultimately, I decided I was too interested in what she wanted to reveal to walk away, although I still wasn't sure if I was truly in my right mind.

Okay, I answered, *What would you like me to see?*

She smiled so wide I could see every tooth in her mouth and then replied, *I invite you to close your eyes or find a spot with eyes open to have a soft, steady gaze.*

I placed my hairpins on the counter, let my arms rest comfortably at my sides, and closed my eyes.

She continued, *Now I invite you to take three deep belly breaths and allow your body to relax and let go of any tension.*

I inhaled and exhaled three deep breaths so that I could feel my stomach fully expand and contract.

Then, she said, *I'm going to guide you through a visualization exercise if that is alright with you.*

I nodded in agreement, and she continued,

As you fall into regular breathing, I invite you to go back in time to what you remember to be your very first memory. And as you go back to your first memory, I invite you to recall as much as you can. What were you wearing? What was it like outside? Was it dark or sunny? Hot or cold? Who was around you? What was going on in your life at that time? Was this a happy memory or a sad one?

And as you envision your first memory, begin to fast-forward through time to about twelve years of age. And as you recall this period, reflect, and sit with those memories that bring you joy and those memories that might still bring discomfort. What was it like to have first days of school or summertime with family? Who were the people that nurtured and guided you? What were you like as a child? Were you shy or opinionated? Were you the class clown? Who were your best friends? What were those moments that still make you cringe in embarrassment? How did you begin to see yourself fitting in the world around you?

And as you recall those special moments from childhood, the ones that made you who you are, continue to move through time to your teenage years. Maybe at the beginning of this time you're beginning to experience your body, and everything around you, changing. What did those transformations feel like? How did you experience them? Were they terrifying, scary, or exciting? What did you take with you from childhood and what did you leave behind? What were you beginning to care about? How was your identity shaped and molded? Who did you want to be when you grew up? What were you preparing for as you got older? What scared you about becoming an adult? How did you experience relationships and love? What did you define as your purpose and passion? What caused you to say, "I can't believe I did that?"

I invite you to fast-forward to adulthood. How did you begin to find comfort in who you are? How did you begin to define love and family? What caused you to shift and change? Continue to reflect on your life up until right now and think about those different versions of you that got you to this moment. Breathe into those parts that feel joy, love, pain, and discomfort, and when you're ready, open your eyes.

As my eyes fluttered open, everything around me was brighter, and a deep sense of calm settled within me. Then my reflection said,

Look at me. Who do you see?

Miraculously, my reflection transformed into a collage of many different faces appearing all at once before coming together as a singular image.

I see me, I answered, *And I see her . . .*

. . . in the depths of
my heart's story

When Love Wouldn't Let Me Alone

I was immediately drawn
To his magnetic energy
Which amplified my pulse.

We'd known each other for years,
First meeting while he dated
A friend I no longer know.
They didn't work out.
Yet I stepped back, not wanting
To cross an invisible boundary,
Determined to be *just friends*.

He remained consistently by my side,
Coloring outside the lines
Of the mundane aspects of my life,
Making them even more beautiful.
His presence was nourishing
In all the right ways.
I caught myself falling,
A little afraid.
So I denied and resisted.

He caught himself falling too,
And professed and persisted,
Drawing closer and closer,
Until his lips embraced mine.
Everything fell away
As we fell into each other.

The fluidity of love's magnitude
Was revealed
In the purity
Of our connection

For us to see each other
In the glow
Of imperfect perfection
While standing
In the fullness of our power.

Based on the story of Anonymous

Me, Him. Mom, Dad.

When we fight,
We yell with
Recklessness,
Slam doors until
Kitchen cabinets shake,
And tear off
Each other's band aids
To reveal deep, open wounds
Which started off
As paper-thin cuts.

Then we laugh and carry on
As if nothing were
Ever wrong
In the first place
Or second place.
I don't like the topsy turvy
Nature of our love,
But it's comfortable.

My parents came to visit
Just a few weeks last summer.
As Mom and I caught up over
Cigarettes and a bottle of wine,
She casually observed,
"He's a lot like your dad."

It's true.
They laugh at similar jokes
Love the same sports teams,

And get cranky when they don't
Get a full eight hours of sleep.
One evening, out to dinner,
An argument erupted
Between my mother and father.

It was savage and unexpected.
My husband turned to me
And whispered, *Just like us.*

Based on CF's story

When I Thought He Was "The One"

He was that church boy next door whose attention made me write his name in my journal over and over again until it became mine. Everyone just knew we were a perfect match made in the pews. I knew it too. I met him at seventeen, and he was everything I wanted in a boyfriend and future husband. He and I were to marry and have this idealistic life with all the bells and whistles. I figured I was ready for that, and I imagined he was too. He was my first love, and I couldn't envision my life with anyone else but him. So much so that I ignored the signs revealing who he truly was as my naivete shrouded me in a rose-colored hue.

I grew and grew, and he didn't like it at all. He resented me for my achievements because he had very few of his own. I know that now, although I didn't know it then. I had an exciting internship while he found his way into the wrong crowds. I was accepted into college, and he was expelled from school during our senior year, unable to graduate. I had loving family support. He didn't. However, I foolishly hoped my love might save him, and success would be motivating.

I wanted to take on his burdens and give him my everything and, in many ways, I did. He was my first. We only did it a couple of times because, according to Christian doctrine, sex outside of marriage makes you impure. I wanted to preserve whatever I could. I rationalized our intimacy by telling myself I was fornicating with the one I was to spend the rest of my life with. My young mind didn't know any better.

Unexpectedly, he changed and became distant, just as everyone warned. He moved forty-five minutes away and stopped calling me as often. I fell from number one on his Myspace "Top Five" to fourth place. He also adopted new "friends" into his inner circle. He called them his "little sisters." Every time I confronted him, he said nothing was going on and accused me of not trusting him. I started skipping my college classes to make the long drive to see him and prove to him that he still had a loving girlfriend. Though it didn't make up any lost ground between us.

One day, a mutual friend told me she saw him at the club with one of his "friends," carrying on and looking like a couple. I confronted him about it and, of course, he lied. He said he was picking up one of his guy friends and not to worry. I gave him twenty-four hours to come clean and, when he didn't, I ended the relationship. Honestly, it was a relief not to have to try anymore. Still, my heart was broken, and I cried for an entire month. At the time, I thought he was The One.

Based on the story of Anonymous

A Word for My Very Late Boyfriend

I waited impatiently for you
To pick me up from work.
I was weary and wanted
To prop my aching feet on the couch,
To rest in front of the TV.

You were running beyond late.
Twenty minutes became an hour.
You sent my calls to voicemail
And left my texts unread.

I knew when you finally showed up
You'd find a way to make it all my fault.
It's hard for you to accept responsibility
For the ways in which you hurt me.

I love you in contempt of myself
But there are days when I don't like you,
Days when reciprocity runs low,
And my, "How was work?"
Is met with a "Good," followed by silence.

Or when your ego makes you believe
You can do no wrong, even as I pull away
After some passive aggressive comment you've made.

Or when you're too blind to see
That I sacrifice to do for you
What you wouldn't do for me.

I know you don't
Mean me harm,
But at times I wonder
If you mean me well.

Reminding you to sometimes say
"Hey babe, you look nice today,"
Turns into a one-sided fight,
Because you get upset with me
For seeming upset with you.

Will we ever see eye to eye?

Whenever you make me cry,
You give me space
In the place of apology,
Leaving me unreconciled.

I simply desire that you
Listen to and acknowledge me
Rather than take me for granted.

Although my heart hurts,
It wants us to work, to try.

I'm getting so tired
Of expecting you to arrive.

Based on the story of Anonymous

My Stubborn Ways

She wanted us to move in together and was actively trying to have a baby. I feared losing my independence and falling victim to societal expectations to settle down and have a "conventional sort of life." I didn't want to live with her. I didn't want to live with a partner, period.

As someone who grew up in the suburbs, I came to believe that the nuclear family perpetuated isolationism, contrasting with my firmly established value of community. So, despite being with her for years, part of me continued to be non-committal and resistant to the ways she wanted our relationship to change. I told her to break up with me. She became pregnant very soon after we called it quits. I think she was able to finally conceive when the halo of my inflexibility was no longer an obstacle.

We were broken up for quite a while but remained very close. Over time, I realized how much I longed for there to be an us. One day, I invited her out for coffee and blurted out, "I think I should move in with you." She had a knowing smile on her face, indicating she knew this for a long while and was patiently biding her time until I came to the same conclusion. However, I needed to go through that tumultuous phase to grow into that knowing and become stronger for it. Soon after my declaration, I packed up my single life to create one with her and her child.

While this life isn't easy, it's not horrible like I thought it would be. It's definitely not conventional. In fact, since moving in with each other, things between us have been quite wonderful. So wonderful that this year marks our fifth of loving each other under one roof. There are times when I miss the simple pleasures of single life like having the bed all to myself and moving along at the pace of my own schedule. But if I didn't have this, what she and I have right now, I'd miss her more.

Based on the story of Anonymous

Soap Bubbles in the Sky and My Redeemer

His promises were like soap bubbles floating towards the sky. They were so exquisite in the light of the sun that I was entranced, momentarily ignorant to their impermanence. He promised to show me all the world's vibrant colors and love me until the end of his days. He promised to become my everyone and everything with a set of vows and an inscribed ring that read, "Forever." We started our life together with plans to expand our family. Yet, when our cherished child came, he forever disappeared, and his promises burst into the sky so exquisitely.

I pledged to never again be fooled into love and grew steel armor where once there was softness. For a little over a year, I knowingly acted against my better judgement to escape the grief he sowed into my spirit. I lay with a man promised to another in a meaningless and fleeting indiscretion. He said he was going to break it off with her, but I didn't care. I was in rebellion against love and all that it stood for. I believed every man only wanted to get from me what he could and said to myself, "If I'm going to be used, I might as well get something from it too." I abused my body with late nights filled with alcohol and bad decisions, because I didn't believe in its value. I became so numb to the sensations of my dreams and desires, it was as if they didn't exist. It was as if I didn't exist.

Thankfully, I was saved from my reckless impulses. It so happened that whenever I closed my eyes to sleep, a cloudy vision would come more and more into focus. Through the cover of darkness, I saw from afar the light of my child's eyes beckoning me. I drew closer to its glow, allowing her to guide me home where I will forever remain, for richer or poorer, in sickness and in health. Her life has made a way for a lasting love to sprout through my heart's cracks and crevices and grow into the lushest of gardens. This love has swept me off my feet, broken through my armor, and delivered me into a most holy and unbreakable covenant.

Based on the story of Anonymous

The Language of My Heart

My mind, afraid of vulnerability,
Can never seem to interpret
The language of my heart into words
Leaving me tongue-tied.

Yet his careful attentiveness gently cradles my fears
And helps my mind translate my heart's expressions.
My burgeoning love is delicately exposed
By utterances that escape my lips in his company.

I savor in the warmth of your smile.
You make me want to sing a love song.
I miss you all the time.
I don't know if we'll last, but I cherish your presence all the same.

Based on Van Nguyen's story

My Relationship with a Narcissist . . .

I knew he came from a winding, complicated road when our relationship began. He experienced a difficult divorce and had a series of challenging relationships afterwards. I didn't rush him towards a forever with me and remained lovingly patient while he fought off his demons. They, whoever *they* are, say patience is a virtue. At some point, it became my albatross.

Our love story consumed most of my thirties and is my longest serious relationship to date. Much of my time with him was spent trying to understand and rationalize his behaviors. Much of his time was spent jerking me around, making me believe in a future he could never give me. He pulled me in so close before pushing me away, only to pull me in close again, then push me away. What a vicious cycle! I endured it because I thought he was wounded and in need of healing, as if my love could transform him from the wild beast into a dotting prince. Really, he was looking to prove that he could have his proverbial cake and eat it too.

I was out and about one sunny afternoon when I saw him holding hands with her. I confronted him about it when we were alone, and he told me she was his business associate. Something about his story didn't sit right with me. I did a bit of online sleuthing and discovered that they were engaged! As I dug even deeper, I found out he was cheating on me with her for at least the last six months of our relationship.

I broke up with him. In reviewing those last six months, I saw with new awareness the red flags I'd originally dismissed and wondered how I was so naive. I always gave him the benefit of the doubt, and he made me out to be a fool. I wondered why he constantly dragged me into his life, and if I was a mere distraction until he found what he was looking for. It was as if he robbed me of an opportunity to find my happiness because he couldn't see past his own selfishness.

What really stung was knowing that she'd reap all the love and hard work I had poured into him, while I was left with little to show for my efforts. Although I know I did nothing to deserve what he did to me, it's hard not to repeatedly replay our relationship in my mind to see what I could've done wrong. At the end of the day, I never asked him for much. All I wanted was for him to love me, want me, desire me, miss me when I was gone, and shield me from harm. Yet how could he protect me from harm when he couldn't save himself from his own demons?

Based on the story of Anonymous

My Many Musings on This Sleepless Night

2:00 A.M.
Sleep is elusive yet again.
I turn and toss and find
No easy place to rest.
I watch his chest rise
And fall, rise and fall.
   Open your eyes.
   See me once more,
I beg him in my mind.
He continues to lie
Too deep in a whiskey slumber,
No longer responsive
To my desires.
I close my eyes tightly
And attempt to shapeshift
Into someone he could love.

2:17 A.M.
I'm still me.
Still awake.
Still anxious.
It took some time for me
To grow accustomed
To the enveloping warmth
Emanating from his body.
He'd rock me in his arms,
Hold me extra close,
And whisper fairy tales in my ear

Until I fell asleep.
I loved how open, vulnerable,
And attentive he was.
Then the earth shook around us,
And his side of the bed turned cold.
I was exiled.

2:41 A.M.
Maybe I'm too much for him.
He always says
I overthink things
And need to calm down.
I can't help that I feel things so intensely.
Maybe I'm not enough.
His withholding reminds me
Of my mother.
She always takes away her love
More quickly than she gives it.
I still think about whether I am,
Or ever was, wanted by her.

2:55 A.M.
He gives me so little.
He doesn't wonder about me
And rarely asks about my day.
It's like he's become a hollow shell,
But he's right here.
I've had huge meltdowns in his presence.
Yet he's always stayed and never
Demanded that I go.
Things might return to how they once were
If I could be more solid and peaceful.

3:13 A.M.
I'm entirely exhausted.
I must sleep.
Soon, a new day will begin.

Based on Wendy's story

My Intoxication

The way her dark hair sways along
The middle of her back is a song
I hum when no one's listening.

One drink and then another.
One smoke and then one more.
I'm in complete and total love with her—

The shape her lips assume
When she's in thought, I want to kiss them
And caress her beautiful, troubled soul.

Oh no!
Oh no!
Oh no!

Oh! These feelings of intoxication,
I've never felt them before.
I try not to feel at all.

One more drink and then another.
One more smoke and then one more.
I'm trembling in fear of such a powerful desire.

But damn it! I just can't help myself.
I've tried.
I've tried.

I've tried to capture
The sound of her laughter in words,
But I'm taunted by my futile attempts.

She taunts me in her freedom of expression.
I want that for myself. I want to be as I am.

Yet I walk through life wearing a suit
That doesn't fit. It's so uncomfortable,
Because it was never made for me.

I wear it even as it slowly suffocates
All the life from me.
I pray she'll grant my reprieve.

Whenever I look into her eyes,
I know I'll be saved
As I drown in their unrequited pools.

I don't want to die a false version of myself.
One last drink, and then I leave here.
One last smoke and then, no more.

Based on VS's story

My First Love,
aka The Boy Across the Street

It's funny how one minute in life can open a door to a space in your soul that's so big the entire multiverse can pass through it. One Saturday morning, I woke up with sleep still in my eyes. I didn't want to move from the comfortable nook in the corner of my bed which was fitted to the exact shape of my body. I knew if I did, I'd have to fight my kinky, natural hair, which was a daily process. Yet that day, I was resolved to tame it. I made my way into the shower and let the warm water dance on my scalp and bead in the tight, onerous strands.

I decided to let my hair dry into a shape of its own making while I relaxed with a bowl of Cap'n Crunch, Saturday morning cartoons, and music videos. I massaged Noxzema on my face for good measure to complete my morning of beauty. Suddenly, my mom's voice said, "Get dressed. We goin' to help my coworker who's movin' in across the street." I didn't want to go but couldn't deny my mother's request. In silent rebellion, I put on my shoes and trudged to our new neighbor's house with Noxzema on my face and my hair in disarray. I didn't give a care in the world for what my mother or her coworker thought of me.

I saw him as he lifted a box from his porch. It was as if time stood still and didn't resume until he looked at me, smiled, and waved. "Whoa," I said to myself, "*Who* is that?" Something about his spirit connected with mine and took my breath away. A beautifully electric sensation charged across all of me. Without one word, I turned around and ran into my house to wipe away the face cream, style my hair and change into an outfit that was a statement of who I was. I wanted so badly for him to see me. From that moment on, he treated me as a friend and got to know me as I got to know him. We spent hours talking about everything under the moon. I remained infatuated.

I was incredibly sad the day my mom told me that we were moving to a nearby town. Although it was only twenty-six miles away, the distance felt like it was hundreds since neither of us was able drive to see each other. I couldn't drive, and he didn't have a car. As my family packed up our car and prepared to drive away, I saw a remnant of myself sitting on his porch's step, caught in the light of his smile. I never forgot about him. His loss from my life was like a phantom pain from a limb I yearned to reattach, even as life carried me away to new places, adventures, hardships, mistakes, and lessons. I dated other men, but no man measured up to my memory of the boy who used to live across the street.

Although much time had passed, I couldn't get him off my mind. I decided to find his number and gathered all my courage to call him. When he didn't pick up, I left him a message filled with anticipation. "Hi. I don't know if you remember me. I used to live across the street from you. Our mothers worked together. Anyway, you crossed my mind and I wanted to reach out. This is my number. Call me back." Several days later, my phone rang, and when I answered, his voice was on the other end. My heart beat away from my chest with a loud boom, boom, and something inside of me was restored. "Hi. Yes, I remember you," he replied, "It is so good to hear from you. What have you been up to? How is your family?"

After that call, we talked almost every day and became friends again. One day, I admitted, "You know, I had a massive, embarrassingly big crush on you since the first day I saw you." He replied in surprise, "Really! I didn't know. I wish I knew." We both agreed that we would go on a date the next time I visited family down home. I wanted to see if my feelings were a fanciful girlhood crush about someone I had idealized, or if they were more. The next time I went home, I called him and nervously said, "I'm here."

On the evening of our first date, I changed outfits a hundred times trying to find the right look. When he picked me up, I felt like that little girl all over again, waiting for the boy I liked to look up and notice me. After dinner and a movie, we went back to his place. We didn't have sex, although I once again experienced that electric sensation throughout my entire body. It escaped into the air and crackled. I was terrified to kiss him because I knew it wasn't just a girlhood crush. It was this beautiful, innocent, enduring, passionate love. I knew that even as a little girl, my spirit recognized him as its medicine. If I kissed him right then, I wouldn't be able to bear being apart from him. I had to leave him so I could get back to a life I'd painstakingly created for myself, and he could not come with me because his roots were embedded in the land of my hometown.

Every time I visited home, I had to see him. We were pulled to each other like planets orbiting the sun. Each time we saw each other, one of us was in a relationship with someone else, but the love I had for him continued to be a strong presence in my life. One day I told him, "It's not just a crush, it's love," and his response was, "I imagine that a relationship between you and I would be one of the most powerful things I could ever experience in my life." Sadly, we couldn't be together. We didn't even discuss a relationship after he said that, but he knew I loved him, and I knew he loved me.

It was a bright summer day when he told me he met someone new. He wasn't sure if it could become serious, but something about her sounded different from other girls he once dated. As soon as I met her, I could tell she didn't like me. It seemed she was threatened by my close friendship with her boyfriend. After my first and only meeting with her, I couldn't reach him, no matter how many times I called or how many messages I left. It was as if we'd been disconnected. That year, I drove to my mother's home on a cold and rainy Christmas day with the hope that he'd be waiting for me when I walked through the door. Instead, there was a message, "*Call me, Love T.*"

I was angry, confused, and hurt that after he had shut me out of his life, he had the audacity to request that I call him. But I called him. "She's pregnant," he whispered. There was a subtle ache in my womb. He decided to make a life with his girlfriend because she was going to have his baby, and he didn't want his child to grow up without him. He said that would have been the greatest heartbreak of his life. I started to cry so hard my whole body shook. I knew that meant the end of our friendship.

He said, "I will choose my child and will not look back, but for one night I need to be with you. I've got to make love to you." To say I was shocked would be an understatement. We'd only kissed once or twice and hadn't made love because there was no way either of us could cope with the reality of going our separate ways afterwards. I stood numbly in contemplative silence. How could he ask this of me? Could I sleep with him and walk away afterwards? Would I be able to move on from him once we made love? The final realization was that I had no idea what the future held, but I could not miss the opportunity to make love with this man. I softly said, "Yes."

I showered and let the warm water dance on my scalp and bead in the strands of my hair. As I got dressed, tears of joy and sadness fell down my face. I made my way to his place, and when I walked through his door, he looked at me intently for what seemed a lifetime. It felt as if he saw through me to a soul that patiently waited for him. I could tell he'd been crying too, but then he smiled, and it melted away any tension and distance between us. There was only rapture. There was only love. There was only us. It is still one of the most beautiful experiences I've had in my life and the second most heartbreaking.

Years later, I called him. I hadn't seen or heard from him since that night, but his presence was on my mind and in my spirit. His mother answered his phone, and my heart skipped a beat. "Oh dear," she said, "He has passed away. He had an asthma attack and couldn't be saved."

I couldn't breathe.

A door opened into a huge space within me.

Time collapsed in upon itself, and I saw the two of us walking hand-in-hand through a field of purple flowers. Our little boy was nestled against my breast, and when he looked up at me, he smiled his father's smile. As I returned to this reality, I knew our love was transcendent, and we were still a possibility.

Based on NAF's story

The Way He Holds Me

I previously existed
As a ghost haunted
By broken lovers' pasts.

And I was lonely,
So very lonely,
Even though I wasn't alone,

Until I sacrificed my pain
To love's true nature and experienced its grace
With acceptance and surrender.

To be held by my love.

He holds me in such a way
That I can live openly
Because my existence matters.

Happiness lives within the sanctity
Of this union,
Granting me corporeality.

My scars have light and air to breathe.
They have begun to disappear,
Becoming less a part of me.

Today, I give thanks for having been awakened
By his healing touch as he whispered, *I love you*,
With the rising sun.

Based on MM's story

. . . in my yearning
for home

When Home was Lost to Me

Home. There, each day had a particular peace that crafted meaning into existence. The buildings were new but the community, familiar. I was surrounded by open, green fields as far as the eye could see. I often ran through them with abandon. Small pieces of my heart were left in those blades of grass which often tickled my bare feet. The air was invigorating as the musk of nature commingled with fresh, clean breezes. When the sky was blue, it went into eternity until bright stars glittered in the night.

Home. It was not too big or too small. I had the right amount of room to breathe, stretch out my arms, and embrace the freedom of being, no matter the constrictions of my parents placed upon me. They had expectations of me based on their traditional ideals of what a young Indian girl should be which never aligned with my personal truth.

However, I could manage that stress from my parents because I had community. My teachers honored my spirit. I found constant restoration in friends who bore gifts of acceptance and pure compassion, and was blessed with healing through music that sprang from my fingertips onto a waiting instrument. I played the songs of each blade of grass and was content.

Then, everything was different. My parents decided to move before my ninth-grade year, and home was torn away from me and replaced with stale, cold air, and grey, narrow spaces. I changed states between the several hundred miles between home and this new beginning—from hometown girl to foreigner. I was out of place in a land where elitism ruled every interaction, and people were automatically given labels. Rich. Poor. Gifted. Talented. Average. This. That. The other. I was miserable.

I dreaded going to school, and I dreaded being alone with my parents. I was so lost. I escaped through the pages of my favorite books and found refuge in making music with the orchestra. These things brought me the greatest comfort when I didn't fit in with any clique or crowd and home seemed unwelcoming. Yet no story or sheet of music could stop my spiral into depression. I had no safe place to exhale and moved through life as a sight unseen, pining for wide blue skies and those green blades of grass.

Based on VS's story

Me, the Perpetual Stranger

What was to be a year
Became a lifetime
Of separation from
The noise,
The colorful festivity,
The smell of pungent spices
Wafting from Auntie's kitchen,
Cousins diligently looking
For me in our games
Of hide and seek,
Uncle teasing Mom
About something from their
Childhoods . . .

The joy of being with,

Then suddenly, without.

Uprooted and carried
To a far and away place.
Mother, Father, Brother,
And me.
Strangers in a foreign land
Without family.
Replanted in an unfamiliar soil
That could never be native.

They promised the change
Would be good.
They were wrong.

The everyday realities
Crafted in Auntie's kitchen
And my secret hiding spots
Turned to sepia toned memories
That will forever evoke joy and
Tender sadness.

Devastation
Marked my perception
With no one to understand
The subtle nuances
Of my origin.
Transformed
Into a lonely outsider,
Never quite fitting in with
Those who looked like me.
Their silences asked me,
"Why do you speak our language
Like that? Are you one of us?"
Their steady stares told me
I wasn't.
Stark differences in culture
Magnified why I didn't belong.

My roots still need the proper soil
To spread themselves through the nurturance
Of family and community, but I find myself
The perpetual stranger, and now I've been
Gone from home for so long, it's no longer known to me.

Based on the story of Anonymous

A Five Dollar Bill and My Image in the Mirror

I drew pretty pictures for the American couple sitting next to me on the airplane and practiced speaking to them in English. They gave me a five-dollar bill for some ice cream. I placed it in my pocket. People sat on the cabin floor, which was unrefined and very un-European. From the window, the world was big and yet so very small. Finally, descent. Excitement coursed through my ten-year-old body. New home, new life, new country, for Mom, Dad, my brother, and me. Strangers in a foreign land now called *home*. When we landed, I placed the five dollars in my mother's hand. As we deplaned, I braced myself for the impact of the unknown.

We stayed with my aunt and her family. I still see that neighborhood vividly in my mind's eye. It was different than I thought it would be, and I stayed quiet as I adjusted to a new way of being. I constantly marveled at all the people everywhere. They moved fast, even when they had nowhere to go. Immigrants. Some like me, others not like me at all, speaking a myriad of mother tongues that swirled around me in a symphony of accents and intonations. And all the name brands felt overwhelming and unnecessary. They were stamped everywhere, from people to buses to billboards. It was as if society constantly fed itself off blatant consumerism.

When I started school, the principal placed me in the fifth grade. I had already completed it. I couldn't speak English, so had to take it again. I walked into my classroom full of verve and confidence which was broken down by the kids on the playground over time. They made fun of me for being an immigrant, my broken English, caring about grades over popularity, not having money, etc. Implicit signs told me to feel bad about being my natural self. It seemed like I was a first-class swimmer, facing large waves, furiously trying to swim against the current, never getting anywhere.

In those moments of insecurity, I'd visit my image in the mirror and recall the reflection I saw in it before our great move. It was my last day at school and my fifth-grade class threw a going away party for me. Mom did my hair specially for the occasion, and let me wear stockings and a short skirt that my aunt had sent from the U.S. That day, I liked the way I looked. I liked my body. I liked my face. I liked the idea that I was becoming more mature in a transition to womanhood.

When I arrived at school, two boys, one whom I had a crush on, met me in the hallway, made a swing with their arms, and carried me to class. It was as if they were acknowledging my beauty. I liked that, too. As this new acknowledgment of my divine femineity emerged, I increasingly looked forward to nurturing it in a different place. I'd have an opportunity to experience another version of me while living in the promise of America's dream.

Based on Sasha Zolley's story

My Solitary Bus Ride

I boarded the bus on the first day of sixth grade with a brick in my stomach. It was taking me, and many other middle-schoolers from my part of the city, to a lily-white school in the suburbs, forty-five minutes away. I immediately knew I didn't fit in with the other kids on the bus. I was "too white" for them, and they saw me as the prim, proper, soft-spoken biracial girl from around the way.

I didn't know where to sit, and all the familiar faces were suddenly strange. Everyone seemed to have a group that they belonged to, and loud chatter filled the air. As the bus pulled away from the stop, I stumbled to the back where there was an empty seat and longingly looked out of the window, pining for yesterday.

Before the sixth grade, I went to a magnet elementary school that was a pebble's throw from home. Its ins and outs were familiar like the back of my hand. I had been there since kindergarten, and it became my safe place to be a regular kid when growing up in my neighborhood didn't always feel easy. When I was in elementary school, it didn't matter so much that my clothes were hand-me-downs and not name brand, or that my parents were working poor. What mattered was that my teachers cared about me, I did well on my assignments, and expressed myself creatively.

Each day, I'd walk my younger brothers to and from school. We always looked forward to the last bell of the day because then we, along with a small group of kids from the block, could go to someone's house to play fun games until our parents came home. Life had a certain inexplicable ease which disappeared as soon as I boarded that bus.

As I walked through the doors to my new school, I realized I was "too black" and "too poor" for the privileged white kids who all appeared to know each other from way back when. I could feel their eyes judging the way I looked and dressed and became self-conscious and hyper-aware. Suddenly, it mattered that I was wearing off brand hand-me-downs and came from a working class, predominantly black neighborhood. From that first day on, I struggled to find my place while navigating disparate realities.

I was unacknowledged and unclaimed by the black kids to the point of invisibility. At the same time, the white girls, who moved through life with an air of perfection, continuously bullied me into doing things in exchange for their friendship. They always laughed at me for being so gullible as to think they'd be friends with me. Yet I knowingly fell for their tricks each time because I hoped that one day someone would accept me. Whereas in the fifth grade I was on the honor roll, I failed almost every class in the sixth. It's not that I couldn't do the work. I just stopped paying attention. My childhood innocence was lost to me, and I was unpopular, alone, and so far from home.

Based on Kelsey Norton's story

My Name Written in the Sand

I sought to flourish
Some place new
For different scenery,
A fresh perspective,
And mountains in view.

I moved to an enchanted wonderland
Where hilltops were quilted in delicate snow
Replacing what I used to know—
The white noise of blue-green foaming waves
And endless warmth radiating from the sun
Like love from my mother's eyes.

What was fresh swiftly became old,
As my bones became chilled from the unforgiving cold.
I desperately yearned to return home,

To live as if nothing had changed.

And I could find my name
Written in cursive inside of a heart
On ocean kissed sand.

Based on CF's story

. . . in the pain that made me

*(**Self-care advisory:** Pieces in this section cover topics related to abortion, childhood abuse, intimate partner violence, sexual assault, and suicide. These have an asterisk of indication next to the titles.)*

The Storm Inside Me

A storm collected inside me,
Causing waves
Of the great ocean
To crash against
Forgiving rocks.

The water was salty,
Salty and bitter,
Bitter and sweet
Like my tears
Which fell mightily
As heavy raindrops
In mutiny from
The sky.

I wanted him to see me,
To notice
I was not okay,
I was not alright,
Because those tears,
They were falling down
While the storm
Thundered, raged,
And clapped.

Without looking up
From his evening paper
That he carefully read
At the dinner table,
He said to me,

Oh darling, please,
Straighten your back
And put those tears away.

He refused to create
A holding space
For my cries,
So I sat up straight
And wiped the wetness
From my face.

I stayed silent.
I sat stoically
While my insides twisted
And my soul burned.

Now, I quietly wonder,
Where do young girls go
When they want to release
Their unshed tears?

Do they offer them
To an endless ocean
Whose waves crash
Against forgiving rocks?

Based on the story of Anonymous

To My Dear One*

You often tried and put your arms
Around me in attempts to draw me into
The intimacy of fellowship.

I froze.
Skin grew cold.
Breath became shallow.
Little hairs on my arm stood at attention.
I'd try to escape my body—

"Please don't touch me!"
I screamed internally in the voice
Of a little girl, just turned five.

I desired to push you far, far away
So air could return to my lungs,
My throat wouldn't feel uncomfortably tight,
And sensation would return to my fingers and toes.
I always wanted to run but would remain
Stuck in place, confused, and horrified.

I want you to know it was never your fault.
It's his.
I thought he loved me and would never hurt me,
Until he did,
And did,
And did
When the sun set into night,
And no one was around to hear my cries.
In the light of day, they didn't see I'd changed,
No longer a little girl just turned five.

They said I was his favorite,
Because he showered me with undivided affection.
In reality, he was stealing away
The best parts of me—
Joy, childlike wonder, an ability to trust—
Even as he placed candy pieces
In the palm of my hand.

Shame made me hide his secret.
I worried they would say I was to blame
Or wouldn't believe my truth as the
The only one that mattered.
No one knew a monster paraded in their midst,
Dressed in the clothing of a most gentle man.

It wasn't until my body transformed
In the first spring of my womanhood
That his attention waned,
But his damage was wrought.

I was free, but I wasn't free.

One day, I looked in the mirror, trying to find
That little girl just turned five.
She was someplace safely hiding,
And didn't want to come out.
Nevertheless, her pain became
The center of my universe
And the lens of my sight.
I couldn't open to love and its touch
But longed to be held in its safety.

At this moment, in the urgency of right now,
The core of me demands to be whole.
And so, I call out her name.

I call out her name.
I call out her name.

I send that pain to the periphery of my vision
To live a life promised to her before she was born.
And, while those wounds will remain in partial view,
I'll deny her no longer.
Rather, I'll climb to the summit
Of what she longs for me to heal.
It's not insurmountable, for she has seen me
Through the darkest of nights,
and I'm here
To stand in her light and reveal all that I am.

My dear one, please embrace me once again
So I may share my warmth.
It was never your fault.

Based on Van Nguyen's story

My Night of Blackened Memories*

Late night drinks
Between friends.
Diminished awareness
Of what was what
And who was who.
A haze settled into the air.

That night moved
In fast flits and flickers.
I tried to slow it down
And anchor myself
To each second
Passing me by,
But I couldn't hold on
To anything.

I needed to make
The short walk home
And sleep it off.
Although I don't recall
Drinking much,
My mind swirled
In endless circles.
How I ended up at his place
A mile and a half away,
I'm not sure.

Late night smokes
Between friends.
Lowered cognizance

Of time, distance, and space.
Haze constricted the air.

I floated
In
And out
Of blackness.

What I remember,
I'd like to forget.
What lies beyond consciousness,
I struggle to bring to the front of my mind.

All I know is,
A friend turned fiend
And robbed parts of me
To do with as he pleased.

I couldn't say no to him
And was unable to stop.
My body moved in ways
That betrayed my mind and spirit.

Then the morning arrived.

In a daze, I put on my clothes
And quickly set off home
In confusion and shame.

Why did I go out last night . . .?
I should've gone straight home . . .
I shouldn't have been drinking . . .
I thought I could trust him . . .

I . . .
Never . . .
Wanted it . . .

Based on Tay's story

My Will and Restraint

I walk this earth
As a Goddess
Betrayed,

The pain of it
Too much to bear.

I closed parts
Of my mind to forget
The depths of my magic.

What remains
Is a fiery fury,
Burning brightly,
Ever so sound
In the lonely quiet.

Rage tempts me
In its pure inhibition.

I fight to tame it
Or transform
Into a remorseless creature.

When it's hurt,
Its flames ignite
At the bottom of my voice
As it readies to let out a dragon's
Breath that obliterates,
Destroys, cleanses
To ashes and smoke.

But I extinguish
Through troubled silence
While bequeathing smiles
Upon friends who throw
Darts at my back, use my love
For personal gain, sign their names
Across my talent, and sweetly
Lie to my face. They don't see

How they're saved
By my will and restraint.

Based on the story of Anonymous

What I Don't Want to Miss*

"We love you!" shouted my classmates as I crossed the school parking lot toward my first period class. Someone who I thought never paid me much attention ran up to me and gave me the biggest hug. I thought I'd melt into a puddle in her arms. Instead, I clung to the sound of her soft, soothing voice. Everyone at school, from every social group, held me gently in compassion and care. They knew I had experienced a soul loss.

That morning, I woke up numb. My movements were on autopilot as I got dressed, put books in my backpack, and quietly ate breakfast. I couldn't speak to my mom or dad or sister. They didn't seem to understand how broken I was. As I set foot outside of the house, I put on sunglasses to hide my reddened and puffy eyes. I was surprised to see four of my closest friends parked in the driveway, waiting to drive me to school. Even now, years later, I feel immense gratitude for those friends who waited patiently for me the morning after I experienced one of the most devastating nights of my life.

As we drove to school that day, I lay my head on the cool window to temper flashes that replayed over again in my mind.

There was a loud knock at the front door.

Mom called me downstairs.

There were police officers.

They told me that my best friend completed suicide, and I was mentioned in his letter. I fell to the floor in a flood of tears. I wanted them to carry me away from reality. I sobbed until the sun rose and tried to make sense of what seemed illusory, even as I pieced together memories of him and sealed them into mind. I finally fell asleep for what felt like minutes to wake up remembering that he was gone.

At his funeral weeks later, his mother approached me, grabbed my arms, and asked me, "What did we miss? What did we miss?" That question continues to unsettle me. He had so many spiritual, philosophical, and ethical questions about life that troubled him and was often unhappy. I wonder if I was too caught up in my own life to see him slowly slipping away. I don't recall what I was doing when he decided to transition into a spirit of the unseen realms. And I can't help but feel guilt for not being there to put my arms around his pain and hold him close to me.

Not a day passes that I don't think of him. He gave me a new awareness of love that comes from an understanding of and appreciation for the shared human experience. On rough days, his memory reminds me to look beyond, be mindful of my impact on others, and theirs upon me, and to listen to what's soundlessly said in pauses and long silences. I don't want to miss it—whatever *it* is that could cause a dear someone to see life as too unbearable to live.

Based on Jamie's story

I Survived Him*

He chose lil ole' me—
The girl whose nose could
Be found in schoolbook crevices,
Working diligently to achieve excellence
While never feeling good enough.
He saw my hidden insecurities
From afar and was instantly attracted
To that wounded part of me
That craved to be seen.

We began our relationship
As lovers do.
Smitten head over heels.
When we weren't together,
I longed to be by his side.
When we were together,
I was captivated by his smile
And the feel of his fingers
Intertwined within mine.

His touch shielded me from worry,
His words were filled
With gentle sweetness.
His suave, confident swagger
Arrested my sensibilities
Until I was unable to recognize
Down from left and up from right.

Through him, I was freed from
Self-imposed expectations

And the constant striving
For absolute perfection.
He didn't care about
Writing papers,
Or studying for tests,
Or making good grades.
When I was with him,
I didn't care either.

Then, I noticed I was chained,
And the texture of his love
Turned jagged and rough.
His touch left
Purple blue bruises across my skin.
His words curdled,
Deteriorating my sense of worth.
His gaslighting shaded my sight,
So I accepted less than
I deserved, believing crumbs
To be fine jewels that glittered and shined.

I feared seeming weak,
A person needing to be saved.
My mouth remained shut.
I assumed the appearance of strength
As spectators gave unsolicited advice.
To stay. To leave.
To *keep it in our community.*
To stop provoking him so much.
No one understood as well as
They thought they did.
Do they ever?

Eventually, I regained my vision
And escaped the well crafted
Maze of his mental prison.
It took time and love for my pain
To be transformed
By vulnerability into power.
It continues to be a work in progress.
I can now say the words
I was unable to utter before
And find my peace in them.
"He hurt me, and I survived him."

Based on AG's story

My Choice*

I dream of her.

I hold her hand
As we board
An empty train,
But then her fingers

Separate from mine
As the doors close.
I turn around,
And she is gone,

Reappearing suddenly
In a distant oasis,
Dressed in brilliant white,
Sleeping peacefully.

I feel her

Within the ache
Of where she once existed
And was becoming
In my hallowed place.

I wish I could
Have known her,
But alas,
It wasn't our time.

I pray to be forgiven.

Based on Tay's story

The Pain that Made Me

Pain.
You're a dear friend.
You're my greatest enemy.

Because of you,
My very blood once turned
Against me.

You invited the cold
To settle into my joints
So I couldn't greet the rising sun.
You caused me to labor with my speech
So I couldn't find the right words.

You attacked aspects of my beauty
When tendrils of my crowning glory
Cascaded down the shower drain.
You made my face unrecognizable,
But for my smile.

To everyone else, I was the same,
Yet I felt the comfort
Of your presence when they couldn't understand
What I was going through.

You were in my fight and the salt
Of my tears as my greatest healer.

You rebirthed me in the depths
Of your fire and initiated me
Into this better version of myself.

I thought I'd be swallowed by depression.
Instead I become more of who I am
At the start of every day because I choose
To surrender to your mighty lessons.
I honor you as the pain that made me.

My sincerest gratitude.

Based on Britteney Bass's story

. . . in my everyday
fight to be enough

Where I Stand

I've stood here for quite a long time,
Surrounded by the rustling sound of trees
Where shimmers of light
Bounce across shadows
To caste half-moon kaleidoscopes
Upon the ground.

It's a safe and stalwart place to be.
I don't worry about what's to come
Or what will become of me.
Here I've grown strong and tall,
But every bit of expansion
Has caused this comfortable shadowbox
To become quite small.

When restlessness takes its hold,
I turn in each direction
And see unfamiliar paths
Winding curiously into uncertainty.
I want to know the lives contained
Within their mystery
But wonder if I'd ever find my way back
To this place where I stand.

Based on Ellie's story

My Regret

I ever wasted
Such precious seconds loathing
My fine, rare image

Based on Tay's story

My Everyday Fight

"I'm rubber, you're glue. Whatever you say bounces off me and sticks to you," was a childhood saying that often saved the day when someone said something hurtful or rude. One day in the sixth grade, I wore these khaki-colored shorts which seemed safe and harmless. Nevertheless, as I sat in homeroom, wrapping up some work before my next class, some jackass of a kid pointed at my exposed thighs and loudly whispered to his friend, "Naaaasty!"

My face burned with shame as he and his friend laughed openly at my expense. Although it was just the two of them, it seemed like the entire world was pointing and laughing. I wanted to disappear but acted unaffected. Internally I said, "Oh no," as I instantaneously became glue. That word, and the taunting snickers which followed it, stuck to me. Throughout my youth and young adulthood, all I could see when I looked at myself in the mirror was, "Naaasty!" Now that I am all grown up, that word, although in smaller print, is still glued to me.

Oil of Olay commercials tell me to love the skin I'm in. While it would be great if I could dab night cream on my face to wake up feeling confident and beautiful, loving myself isn't that easy. It takes work and, even on a good day, I'd describe myself more as *cute* than *gorgeous*. On not so good days, I scrutinize the whole of myself and become anxious. Insecurity hangs over my head in a constant cloud.

Maybe if I lived alone on a deserted island, I'd see beauty in my reflection, but I don't exist in a vacuum. Rather, I live in a society where thousands upon thousands of people judge and mentally point fingers at me while calling some aspect of my appearance *nasty*. I don't know if that's true, but that's how it feels all the time. To boot, I'm constantly worried whether I am smart enough or funny enough or cool enough. Beauty is the first domino in the line of aspects of my self-esteem; beauty fell first and knocked the others down one by one. The funny thing is friends, family, and coworkers don't see my looming cloud of insecurity. I'm good at faking confidence, although I feel guilty for being an imposter of sorts.

People don't see that I am constantly on a diet. To be totally honest, I'm at my best at a smaller dress size and like how I look and feel when I'm a little lighter weight. There should be nothing wrong with that, no matter what Oil of Olay commercials say. But I've been losing and gaining ten pounds since that kid made his awful comment about my thighs. That, for some reason, is just very sad to me and distorts my ability to be at home within my own body.

They also don't see how much I seek validation from men, including the bad ones. Men's approval makes me feel more loveable and desirable, but my lack of confidence has made me doubt whether I'll ever meet someone who affirms my worth. This has led to settling. I dated an alcoholic for far too long who often said very mean things to me. My logical brain repeatedly told me, "you deserve better," but my heart expressed the contrary, leading me to believe he was the best I'd get.

Then there was the guy in college who told me that I was *mildly attractive*. I was hurt at first, but then convinced myself being mildly attractive was better than being ugly. Now and again, I've been surprised by a man's interest in me—the kind of man who is too smart and too funny and too attractive. If I'm in a particularly down mood, I'll remember that such-and-such guy liked me, and thought I was cool.

Admitting this is hard and quite painful. Nevertheless, these confessions reveal my truth and my struggle within it. I've stepped onto the road of healing and I'm learning to be more grounded in an unfiltered awareness of myself— untainted by the world's perception. It's a journey that's called on me for quite some time. I hope it leads me down a path of seeing myself as enough, but that's an everyday fight. If only I could be like rubber instead of like glue.

Based on the story of Anonymous

A Symptom of My Hard-earned Success

I'm an imposter,
A complete and total fake.

One day,
They'll all realize
I arrived here by mistake.

They'll see
I'm not as good
Or as talented
As I seem to be.

Based on A's story

My Confidence Undone

Graded by the color of my skin,
Mislead into believing my worth fits
Into a single letter grade followed by plus or minus,
Stymied by an insecurity whispering,
You're not smart enough.

In truth, I know . . .

Who I am,
The power of my intelligence,
And the surety of each step I take.

Until I . . .

Walk into that cold room,
Heels clicking out of rhythm
Against the tile floor,

Sit in that hard, uncomfortable chair
And quietly face the front of the room
Like a soldier at attention,

Look into the eyes of a man
Who takes on the role of oppressor
As he tells us to turn to page thirty-two

And silently acknowledge
The few faces that look like mine.

I want . . .

To rebel against this violent system
Through protest and passive procrastination.

It . . .

Was never built to teach me,
Is the antithesis to my humanity,
And denies me access while demanding
I assimilate or be left behind—*Either way, I lose.*

Outside of that cold room I learn . . .

In vibrant colors
That fill every corner of my universe
With pinks, purples, blues, and greens,

Through barefooted dance
That connects me to the earth,

And in the booming echoes
Of the sacred drum.

Based on the story of Anonymous

The Invisible Dunce Cap which Graced My Head

The music thumps: *boom, boom, da da, dee dee, boom, da, dee*. My feet and arms move in syncopation with every note, and my body winds with abandon as I enact a story of my heritage. I fly into the sun of my soul, no longer afraid to emerge from my inner hiding place to feel its warmth. I welcome the steady gazes that witness my unfoldment as I glide across the stage in complete joy.

Prior to this moment, I was too shy and terrified to dance. Back home, friends and family come together to choreograph dances for big events and celebrations. Several years ago, when my sister announced that she was getting married, everyone wanted to come together to create a special dance for her. I refused to do it and thought, "I suck at dancing, and people will make fun of me." The idea of being exposed in such a public way made me feel sick to my stomach. I had grown accustomed to sitting quietly with my head down, out of sight and mind.

When I was a young child, it was safe to be seen. My family has always been supportive, and in school I had a teacher who I loved and who loved me. She would give me little toy gifts and tokens for doing well in school which made me feel proud to be smart. But I started to change when I moved to a secondary school where my mom was one of the headmistresses. "Oh, that's your mom," became a customary phrase that elicited heaviness upon my shoulders. At that time, all everyone could focus on was this very difficult college entrance exam. There was so much pressure to succeed, and even though the exams didn't occur until the eleventh grade, we started to prepare for them as early as the eighth. One day, our teacher decided to give us a pop practice exam, and I did poorly along with everyone else.

My headmistress, who was friendly with my mother, visited our class, appalled at our collective performance. She said we didn't study enough and were going to do miserably on the exam when the time came. She then asked me to stand up, and as everyone's eyes turned to look at me, she said, "I expected better from you." To date, I've never felt as small and stupid as I did then. It was as if she placed a heavy, invisible dunce cap on my head. To make it all worse, I worried that I'd let my mother down. How could a headmistress's daughter fail so badly? I wanted to escape into a tiny, comforting space inside of myself.

Instead, I disappeared into my studies. I never again wanted to be seen as dumb and incapable. I decided to quietly push myself to success, even as my classmates and teachers put me on a lonely pedestal for being a headmistress's daughter. I. Worked. Hard. When I came home from school each day, I unpacked my books and started studying late into the night.

The work paid off when, in the eleventh grade, I received high marks on that very difficult exam. And, upon graduation, I was celebrated as a student at the top of the class in every grade since starting school. However, the pride I had about my academic accomplishments was fleeting as I sacrificed a social life with peers. I strove to be good enough at school but was never good enough to fit in with the crowd. It also seemed that I couldn't have true friendships that weren't cloaked in jealousy about my achievements, and I never found that sweet spot where I belonged. And so, even as I excelled, I hid to be safe from judgement, envy, and prying eyes.

When I went abroad for undergrad, the onerous weight of being a "headmistress's daughter" lifted from my shoulders. I could be more myself with students who were just like me—smart, driven, different. I was less restricted and better able to express myself amongst peers who are still my friends to this day. I was more confident in my own skin because I was able to start with a fresh canvas to paint the next part of my life.

Still, the pressure to show I am good enough persists, and there are times when I feel that invisible dunce cap on top of my head. Those are the times when I grapple with worry that I won't measure up to people's perceptions of me. When those feelings emerge, I fight the urge to grow small inside of myself in self-protection, and I find the internal rhythm to dance and have greater connection to myself—even when the entire world is watching.

Based on the story of Anonymous

My on the Job Struggles

Every day, my office walls
Move one foot closer to each other.

There's less air to breathe
As I straddle between
Hopeful enthusiasm
And acquiescence to the status quo.

At first, I thought I was going to do such good work
Now, I'm not sure.

If I screamed to the executive gods,
WHAT ARE WE DOING HERE?
My coworkers would call me
Crazy Banshee.

Instead, I gently laugh with an innocent smile
To protect their comfort
In "the way we've always done things."

I want to be myself.
Passionate. Driven.
Speak with well-drawn animation.
Talk loudly with my hands.

No one would understand me.

So, I quietly sit in my office
As its corners slowly box me in.

*** Based on the story of Anonymous***

The Unsettled Ruminations of My Mind

Is it out of reach,
The life I dreamed of as a child?

My mind ventures
Into unsettled ruminations—

Will I ever find The One and be married?
Will I ever be a mother?
Will adult realities meet childhood
Expectations with disappointment?

Ugh. I've wasted so much time
Being in love with the wrong one.
When things ended, I started over
With an emotional shortfall that put me in the red.
Why did I stay so long and give up so much?

It's not that I lead
A sad and miserable life.
Quite the contrary.
I live in abundance and have all that I need.
Simultaneously, I feel let down.

I've done everything the right way.
I like to think I am a good person.
I have so much love to give.
So why am I still alone?

I own my home, am well educated,
And have a solid career.
I am proud of all that I've accomplished.
Why does it seem that my successes
Are liabilities to men's egos?

They don't pursue
Meaningful relationships with me.
They want to feel the warmth
And softness of my body
Without seeing me.
They want me to validate
Their cotton candy dreams
Without ever knowing me.

It's terribly confounding
And out of my control.
Love. Relationships. The future—
Puzzles my mind can't quite
Piece together so each question fits
Into a neat and tidy answer.
Even if the puzzle comes together, one question
Would remain . . .

Is it my fault?

Based on the story of Anonymous

My Morning Routine

I'm an other,
Adjusting to what's
Been normalized
Century after century
And born from necessity
To separate
Through lived constructs.

Every weekday morning,
I open my eyes,
Plant my feet heavily
On the hardwood floor,
And slowly move from
Room to room
As I prepare
For the day ahead.

I take in my image
In the hallway mirror,
Reminding myself
I live in a society
That expects
And anticipates my failure,
Quietly waiting for me
To validate its low expectations.

I won't give it the satisfaction.

As I sit down for breakfast,
I read the morning paper

And sip hot coffee.
Afrobeat fills the room
With sound
Until the clock radio blinks
8:30 A.M.
I take a long breath.
Before I leave the house,
I check to make sure
I have everything I need.

ID badge?
Check
Wallet?
Check
Cell phone?
Check
Keys?
Check
Mask to hide my reality?
Check

It isn't enough to be good.
I must be better than good
To be seen as enough.
And so each day,
I strive.
I smile.
I fight.
I excel.
I hold back tears.

I step into the world
In a crisp, smart suit
And stilettos,

Carrying its burdensome heaviness
Like a pack mule.
I am not a spokesperson,
But I am a representative
For those who follow
In my footsteps,
Looking to get even
One toe in the door
Of opportunity.
My presence pushes
That door open bit by bit
To make space for them
To come through.

I sit at my desk in
My spacious, well-lit office.
My diplomas hang
On the wall behind me.
An insecurity that I carry
Is fastened secretly and
Securely up my sleeve.
It reads, "you don't belong here."

Based on D's story

How a Used Car Salesman and My Best Friend Conjured Up the Blues

After our car was totaled in an accident, we went searching for another. The guy trying to sell us on a mid-size sedan stood only a few inches from my face, talking, and talking, and talking. His words grew bigger by the minute, taking up air and space, as I became a triviality. It was obvious I was ready to leave, but, whenever I stepped back, he took a step forward. I wanted to cut him off with a smart, pithy phrase and then go on my merry way but feared it would've been rude. Luckily, my partner eventually interrupted so we could move on with our day.

That sort of thing happens all the time. It's as if some people perceive my energy as so valuable they want it all for themselves. Or they don't value it at all and see it as cheap commodity they can use and use. Regardless, I end up drained. While being talked at by a stranger for twenty minutes doesn't seem like that big a deal in the grand scheme of things, it does validate an internalized message that says, I'm not important enough. If I believed otherwise, I'd be able to speak up for myself to set boundaries.

Inexplicably, that day at the dealership reminds me of my best friend from high school. He'd make these offhanded, off-color comments about my looks and the shape of my breasts. Every time he called attention to my body, I'd become quite uncomfortable and uneasy. But he never knew any of this because I kept my feelings to myself. Although those experiences with my best friend are unlike the one with the car salesman, and with others who vampirize my energy, recalling my silence to his unwanted attention conjures up a similar kind of blues within me. As much as I wanted to, I couldn't tell either of them to stop because it was as if I didn't matter.

I can't pinpoint the exact origins of this internalized message that tells me I'm not important enough. My parents were very loving, and as a kid I grew up in a tight knit, relatively non-judgmental community. No one close to me ever said, "You're insignificant," but something must have insidiously implanted itself inside of my mind to feed constant messages of low self-worth into my subconsciousness. Maybe it was the things I read and saw on TV. Or maybe it was taking note of the types of girls that received attention and realizing I wasn't anything like them. I'm not entirely sure.

Based on the story of Anonymous

I Am . . .

The granddaughter of immigrants
Who spoke little English and arrived
To this land with bright eyes, knapsacks,
And a singular dream.

A beneficiary
Of whiteness
Through the curse
Of passed
Down
Privilege
Shaping my experience
And the world's perception
Of me.

The daughter of parents
Who proudly wore their blue collars
As they denied themselves
Small comforts so my future
Could beam and overflow with possibilities.

A hostage
To the towering,
Hollow gains
Granted
By the color of my skin
Whose truth
Is buried
Beneath
The limited narrative

Expertly written
On my behalf.

Based on the story of Anonymous

The Price My Body Paid

I was unkind to my body for a very long time. I deprived it of its desires, denied its basic needs, and demanded that it fit into unholy standards of beauty. Yet I somehow felt safe in the grueling and unnatural perfection I contorted myself into. In high school, being "pretty" granted young women gold-plated shields of invincibility and societal worth. If a girl wasn't perceived as attractive, she was at risk of being thrown away. I'd already experienced the haunting pain of being disposable and nonessential in my young life, and I couldn't go through that again.

So, I became a successful anorexic and was praised for how fit, toned, and taut my body appeared. This led to a dangerous cycle of reinforcement. Hearing, "You look so good," resulted in an internal monologue that said, "You'd look better if you lost just one more pound or two." No one cared about the withheld nourishment from my body, mind, and spirit. It was my appearance that mattered most.

I attribute this to growing up in a culture of elitism that sprung from patriarchy and white supremacy where an unspoken caste system was the norm, and women's bodies were commodified for the male gaze. The more I controlled my body through starvation, the more powerful, important, and protected I was within that hierarchy. But they were false truths based in a diseased reality, and I experienced my worth in a system meant to harm me. I internalized that harm until it became self-abuse masked as beauty, and I was a hollow shadow of myself. I know now that I was deceived into valuing all the wrong things, and my body paid the liar's price.

Based on the story of Anonymous

What I Left in the Shadows

My children jump into my bed at sunrise
With hugs and hushed whispers,
Gently rousing me to wake.
My love for them anchors me to this reality.
I lie there and wonder if I was meant to be
A mother. I don't know if I am any good at it.
But I do the best I can, even when
It feels like that will never be enough.

I rest my face in the sun's orange purple rays
Peeking through the blinds and close my eyes
To go back to something forgotten.
The clock ticks, slowly inching forward.
I know I'm losing time to find it,
Even as the minutes will soon become hours,
Become days, become years, become a lifetime.
I wander from thought to thought.

The weight of expectation requires I
Become somebody one day.
And so I stand tall
When I want to collapse beneath life's demands,
Because my mind can be an unforgiving place.
My soul wavers between peace and revolution,
What is and what was, who I am and who I'm
Supposed to be,
The desire to be in a position of power
And the discomfort of that responsibility.

Yet I'm too tired to think, to plan, to decide.
Everyone wants answers from me.
They want me to fix it and make it all better.
It's all so exhausting
To give of my energy until drops of it remain,
Only to give from those remains.
I just want to rest here for seconds more,
To go back to that something before time runs out.

And suddenly, a memory flits across my mind.
I'm a little girl playing the piano,
Something I loved and was quite good at
Until I became terrified to be seen.
That's when a switch flipped inside of me
Causing the spotlights to dim into darkness.
That was the time I hid part of myself
In the shadows and walked away.

"Mommy," says my little boy,
"It's time to open your eyes."

Based on A's story

. . . in the multidimensional
and prismatic aspects
of my faith

What I Can't Tell

I crossed the threshold from skepticism
To tenuous belief in the mystical

When burgeoning spiritual realities
Cleansed me in their supernatural rituals.

I can't tell him why or how I'm not the same,
Lest I bear his disapproval and concerned criticism.

Based on the story of Anonymous

I'm from Praka

From time to time, I go to church with my grandma and watch her pray before we light a candle for the health of the living and another for the peace of the departed. Religion connects her to tradition and a sense of home, and attending service with her gives me the heartfelt knowledge of a time before I existed.

As we light candles, I can't resist taking in God's presence. He's in the curvature of the archways, multicolored glass windows, and carefully chiseled sculptures, and sits among us as the caretaking Father who heals and makes everything okay. If I were to sit in another church, God would be something else, as His persona seems to change from community to community.

In a synagogue, God is potentially your next-door neighbor who is bitching about someone showing up improperly dressed. With this God, it's a chit-chat, and He's the guy who always knows the right way to do things, so you just listen to what He has to say. In a Lutheran church, His existence may be felt somewhere in the abstract. And in a Catholic setting, God might be known as a Father who wants atonement in exchange for sin. The list could go on and on.

However, I don't adhere to any religion or believe in God.

I knew that very early on in life and not only because my mom and grandpa were atheists. God has always seemed to be a construct that separates us from, rather than connects us to, our collective humanity. I don't believe a higher power exists outside of our reality, but it is within each of us, waiting to be explored in loving curiosity.

In junior high school, I had a substitute teacher who also taught philosophy at the local college. I often talked to him about metaphysics and shared with him a fictional story of my origins from the planet Praka. "On Praka," I told him, "we are not beings, but balls of energy." Prakians' mission was to send souls to Earth because too many bodies were born without them. Even though that was a tale of my teenage mind, I upheld it as truth and still do. We are glowing balls of energy, fueled by love, connection, and unity.

What if everyone on this planet comes to view God as a glowing ball of energy whose sole purpose is to emanate and disseminate love? What if we all believe that we have that same glowing ball of energy in the core of our beings, connecting us? Maybe then we would all see each other as we truly are and shout to one another in excitement, "I LOVE YOU!"

While it may seem that I dismiss God and religion, I do value and live by the common threads running through each faith—to love, have good character, be kind to yourself, honor your parents, care for your neighbors, and take responsibility for your part in this world. God and religion become entirely inconsistent with my worldview when they are used as weapons of judgement, shame, and separatism. Ultimately, people can use God and religion as tools for love or weapons of fear. I come across people of different faiths all the time who use their belief as instruments of the former.

When I was fifteen years old, I was invited by a Mormon friend to go to Sunday school. I discovered that my visit coincided with a practice done the first Sunday of each month where anyone can speak and address the congregation. I excitedly wrote a speech, and, when I shared it with my friend the morning of, he told me that the speech is a testimonial. "What's a testimonial?" I asked. He replied, "It's when someone affirms the Church of Latter-day Saints."

Every person who addressed the congregation that morning ended with, "And therefore, I affirm that the Church of Latter-day Saints is the one and only true path." I was instantly nervous because the third line of my speech read, "I'm an atheist." Even with that proclamation, my friend and the congregation supported and were accepting of me. They showed me that despite our differences of belief, we were connected by the collective light of our beings.

And so, while I don't have faith in God, I fundamentally believe in people.

Based on Sasha Zolley's story

On Obedience and My Future Flight with God

There's a quirky three-year-old girl playing alone in a sun-drenched attic with her dolls and toys. As she laughs, her colorfully decorated ponytails gently swing from side to side, and her aura radiates joy and unadulterated happiness. She is living in the present, limitless. If she chose, she could sprout generous wings and journey from cloud to cloud.

Instead, she decides to hold an imaginary tea party for Mr. Bear and Strawberry Shortcake, speaking a language that only the three of them understand. In her obedience to being her truest self, she stands at the right hand of God. I lovingly and protectively want to gather her in my arms and hold her close to me. I sigh in silent reverie, yearning to stay there forever. However, I grew up with clipped wings.

When I transitioned into young adolescence, I couldn't make the mistakes of a normal kid or else I'd be labeled a disappointment to my family and community. I had to adopt a mask of staid perfection, even when I wanted to shout at the top of my lungs, "I'M HERE! I EXIST!" Every Sunday, I sat in the pews as any preacher's kid is obligated to do when she's not helping during service with a perfectly ironed dress, neatly coiffed hair, and shined shoes. I diligently listened as my father evangelized the teachings of Jesus Christ and spoke of what it meant to be an obedient child of the Lord.

There were lots of inescapable expectations of obedience from church members, and others in our small community who knew of my father. Eventually, expectations transformed into judgments, and it seemed that the eyes, which should've been watching Him, were always watching the way I walked, talked, behaved, and dressed. Like a chameleon, I adapted to who they wanted me to be to gain acceptance while never realizing my true color. When I was among my friends, I subconsciously reminded myself to have fun, but not too much, and to be a kid but with the moral sensibilities of an adult. The more obedient I was, the more I forgot how to be my natural, quirky self, until one day I no longer found myself on the right side of God.

I learned to put my head down and plow through issues, feelings, and challenges at the expense of connection and self-compassion. I started to shut down to protect myself from whispers and prying eyes. I began a cycle of running myself into the ground to utter exhaustion, trying to prove my value, although I do not know whose approval I continue to seek and why. I'd love to wake up in the morning and say, "Hey queen, you're good enough," but I never do. I want to believe I'm worthy because I was created in His image, but I don't always know that to be true. I pray every day for God to strengthen my wings so I can soar by His side once more and without limits.

Based on the story of Anonymous

My Found Religion

Raised in an agnostic household,
Religion eschewed as a taboo,
A system of manipulation and control,
A toxic medicine to soothe the masses.

My father, born of Holocaust survivors,
Questions the existence of a higher power,
For how could any God allow for the genocide of
    millions?
If there's a God, then only They know.

According to my parents, communal
Places of worship are overly emotional,
And we don't do emotion well.
Crying at the dinner table is forbidden.
Saying what you really think and feel
Leads to awkward avoidance.
Containment is easier than confrontation,
Especially in the face of truth and reconciliation.
Was God there when I wanted to break down in tears,
Silently refusing to reap my parent's pain?
Did They hear me when I went unheard
Or see me when I went unseen?

Maybe there isn't a God.

Yet I find my religion
In breezes that shake seeds from treetops
Onto the waiting, fertile ground,

In the rumbling creek waters
That find river, that find sea,

In the spider's web
Which captures me in its fine tapestry.

Based on the story of Anonymous

On Religion, God, and the God in Me

I don't believe in or trust the Bible. Once I tried to sit down and read it from cover-to-cover. I only made it halfway through the Old Testament before realizing I was reading someone else's truth. I was reviewing often told stories and parables that continue to influence how people blindly perceive and judge me, along with others. I know I am more than what the Bible would make people believe about me, and I am not trying to be what's read in between the lines of that book.

I don't follow any religion. It's a social construct, like race and gender, that requires people to place themselves in a box to avoid judgement, rather than live naturally. I can't help but question the tenets religion perpetuates. Why does it have to be that people must wait until marriage to have sex? We are sexual beings. Why is it taboo to curse when I should be able to express myself as I please? How come I can't show my skin? I love showing my back. It's one of my favorite parts of my body.

I don't have faith in the church, though I grew up in it. I went to Bible camp every summer, and there was always something church related to do. In fact, as a family we spent most of our free time there, sometimes visiting sister churches in neighboring towns. However, something always seemed off and not wholly right when the pastor delivered the Word. I later discovered that he was a predator who abused many of the women of the congregation for years, even as he preached the Bible's messages from the pulpit every Sunday. To this day, there are still people who refuse to receive the Word in that church, and I have trouble believing in an institution that is associated with trauma and abuse.

The church can breed judgmental convictions. I remember a pregnant close friend of the family crying to my mother because, as she was serving food at a neighboring church, a deacon walked up to her, and told her she couldn't be there as she was expecting. She wasn't preaching or giving testimony. She was only trying to serve food. And my son, who has a boyfriend, will miss having family members at his wedding because the Bible says his loving relationship is sinful, and therefore, they can't condone his marriage.

While religion doesn't feel honest. God does. I suppose God is my religion, and my place of worship exists within the core of my being. People see me as gullible. Too trusting. Too loving. Too this. Too that. Always happy and energetic. Always dancing. That's the God in me. God is jovial. God is light. God is running in the sunshine through a field of daisies and tulips on a warm summer day. While I'm human and do not always get it right, God always does. So often, we want to understand the "why" of things. Why did this happen, or that? Why does this exist? Why am I the way I am? Why? Why? Why? But sometimes, I don't need to know. He knows. He always knows.

Because I believe in God's divine plan for us, I am careful about my prayers to him. When I pray, it's not for a specific outcome or to receive some particular blessing. It's to ask that I, and those that I pray for, can handle what God has in store. I ask Him to help us see the path He makes for us and hold it in awareness, and I pray that we can learn the lessons He has created for us so we can have faith in our walks to truth and power. And faith is putting one foot in front of the other, making human mistakes, and trusting that, no matter what, He will see us through.

My connection is with God, and through that I can see and understand myself. He's not what's in that book and neither am I. I am not trying to be. Instead, I am going to be here, working to always get better at living this life. As long as I do that, I will live up to the expectation God has of me, because if I am made in His image, becoming the best me I can be is the closest way to get to Him.

Based on the story of Anonymous

My Marriage as a Reflection of God

One Valentine's Day, I woke up with a card from my husband. As I read it, my heart fluttered down to my fingertips. I appreciated that it could still do that in marriage. He knew all the right things to say and meant every word. I was completely touched by the sentiment of his love.

That day was an incredibly long one, and I finished work later than I anticipated. My husband and I agreed that I'd catch the train home from the city, even though I really don't like taking the train. After such a tiring day, I called him to pick me up. By that time, he'd already made it home, changed clothes and began to relax for the evening, yet he drove all the way back into the city to retrieve me. As we walked through the door, a romantic dinner was waiting. I, however, was exhausted, and I went to bed shortly after we arrived home, sleeping through the remainder of Valentine's Day.

The next day, my husband expressed that although he'd looked forward to spending time with me that evening, he mostly hoped I'd rested well. He knew how hard I'd worked that week. What could've devolved from hurt feelings into a passive aggressive argument was instead one where I was shown just how much I am valued, even when I am not perfect. This is so because God is an ever-present force that sustains the love within my marriage.

To say I knew nothing of marriage before being married is an understatement. When my husband and I underwent marriage prep, a couple in our cohort gave us this book where the first line read, "There's more at stake in your marriage than two people being happy. God's reputation is at stake." That sentence shook me to my core in its weight and heaviness, and I wondered, "How could our marriage be a reflection of God?"

Then I realized, "How could it not be?" God brought my husband and me together which is remarkable because we are opposites in every way. I am an extrovert while he enjoys sitting quietly in solitude. I love talking about my feelings. He hates that. I find peace in a good cry, and he experiences awkwardness in the presence of tears. Yet we complement each other so well in the ways we function and push each other to accomplish things we couldn't achieve by ourselves.

My marriage shows that God never fails and always knows what He's doing, and love is a path of service to the highest power. These core beliefs ease any pressure that could build within my relationship. Rather than focus on being a "good wife," I consider how we can be good people to each other to be good people for this world. Sometimes, it means doing the smallest of things.

I hate folding laundry almost as much as I dislike having to take the train to and from work. My husband, who seems to go through several outfits a day, is the Chief Laundry Creator. One day, he washed all his clothes before leaving for work, and a pile of clean, unfolded clothes sat waiting in the laundry room. Although I wanted to do anything else, I told myself, "suck it up and fold these clothes." I sighed and grumbled as I rolled pairs of socks and neatly folded up shirts. However, my irritation quickly turned to humility when my husband came home and expressed pure joy and relief at having one less thing to do that day. It's moments such as that one, and the slept-through Valentine's Day, which I carry with me when impatience, frustration, or anger want to get the better of me.

My faith in God reveals how I can continuously make my marriage better and blesses me with peace when I don't understand the *why* of things. In times when I am unable to talk to my husband, or when he is unable to talk to me, we both find that we always have a listening ear in God. And, through scripture and prayer, He acts as our greatest counselor. Ultimately, God consistently provides us with a way forward through our love of Him so we can find our way to each other.

Based on AG's story

Does He See Me?

I draw confidence from my faith.

I greet each day
With my shoulders back
And head held high.

I am who the Creator ordained me to be.
No one can take
What God didn't give him
As my value can't be
Commodified in man-made currency,
And the core of my being can't
Be replaced with a false identity.

At times, I wonder if He sees me.
Yet when I falter into doubts
Of whether I will arrive at destinations
Orchestrated by the desires of my mind,
I am reassured by God's word
That my time will come
By the design of His hands.

Then I fall to my knees in worship
And devotional gratitude.

Based on the story of Anonymous

. . . in my reverence
for all my relations

A Song for My Daughter

Born from a womb
Healed through love,
Nursed from a heart
Elevated by her spirit.
I feel peace
And indescribable joy
Because she chose me
To be her mother.
Way down inside,
There's fear, too.

My daughter,
I want to protect her,
I want to save her
From this world
That wants to break her
All the way down
And remake her
In its own image.

She has his nose
And his chin
And his hands,
But my little girl
Has my eyes,
Round, twinkling, curious,
Revealing a soul
Composed of cosmic innocence
And aged wisdom
As if she's been here before.

Her laughter cascades
Into portals of light
Which frees me
From my thoughts,
And her cries resound
In my soul.
She makes new what was old
Through her seeking sight
And reaching hands,
So I experience myself
Anew each day.

My daughter,
I want to protect her,
I want to save her
From this world
That wants to break her
All the way down
And remake her
In its own image.

When I was younger,
I was implicitly taught
That my worth
Was my body—
How it developed,
How it looked,
What it could offer—
It didn't matter
That I was funny
And compassionate.
No one cared that
I was smart.

I want her to know
That her worth
Is invaluable
And inherent.
There's nothing
That can take it away.
I'll forever see her
In her truth
So she can always
See herself.

My daughter,
Can I save her
From this world
That wants to break her
All the way down?
Can I show her
How to faithfully
Love her own image?

Based on Kelsey Norton's story

To My Mama. I Honor Your Hero's Journey

Mama, the world isn't kind to your greatness.
It demands you make yourself small
And disfigures your dreams into delusions.

It uproots the hero's journey from your womb
For you to replant again and again
And shames you into believing
Your strength is a liability.

Mama, I know it pains you to remain here,
Creating miracles from tears
As you lift our burdens upon your back.
So leave, if you must go,
And never forget you're always loved.

When you're ready to return,
I promise to be good.
I promise to be absolutely perfect.
Not a single thing out of place,
And I'll keep a smile on my face
To make you happy.
When dark clouds roll into view,
I'll find harbor in a quiet shelter
Until your storms pass.

Everything will be taken care of.
Don't worry about me.
I've accepted the wisdom

Of the sacred scars and invisible wounds
Inflicted upon your spirit.
I've inherited your strength
To take on this world for us both
And will protect you from a darkness
That doesn't deserve your light or grace.

When you come back to me,
Please stay for as long as you can
And hold my hand
Which always feels so small
In the leathery roughness of your own.
Stand beside me in solidarity,
So I too can bear this weight.

Based on the story of Anonymous

Falling in Love and Coming Out to My Parents

I fell totally in love with a beautiful soul who broke me open wide in profound revelation. It was as if we were birthed from the same fire, but she went her way, and I went mine, forgetting about one another until our paths converged again. Her arrival into my life was unexpected and quite necessary, as she extended my worldview beyond the five senses.

When I met her, I thought I was the only Indian lesbian to ever exist. She proved me wrong and introduced me to other South Asians in the LGBTQ community. What's more, although we met in the Pacific Northwest, we both hailed from the same Indian community in the Northeast. I was astounded that she was out to her parents, and they accepted and loved her. In so many ways she was just like me, and her parents were just like mine. Yet, unlike me, she was able to be more herself with her mother and father. The notion of coming out to my parents was a terrifying one, even though I lived openly within my Pacific Northwest community for over a decade. I assumed I'd have to keep my sexual identity hidden from them forever or face all-out rejection.

At that point in my life, my parents wanted me to be a model Indian American girl who lived in wealth and luxury with two and a half kids and a doting husband. Although I loved my career and lived in a paradise on earth, my happiness never seemed enough for them. I called and visited home less and less over time, hoping to avoid the fifth-degree questions of why I wasn't living up to their idealized version of me. Answering with, "It's because I'm gay," would've put a huge crack in the middle of my very fragile relationship with them.

But the more I fell in love with her and the more I found home in my community, the more I understood how much I desperately wanted what she had—freedom. I couldn't have it until I stopped hiding from my parents. With her loving support, I decided it was time to come out to them. In that decision, I held two things to be true: no matter how far they might push me away, I could never walk away from them, and coming out to them would initiate their journey of having a lesbian for a daughter.

I went home to the Northeast for a Christmas holiday with a plan in place. I called a local friend and asked, "If shit hits the fan with my parents, can you pick me up and let me stay with you until it's time for me to leave?" I mentally prepared, as much as I could, for their reactions. I thought it was going to be bad, even though I couldn't predict how bad it would be. In my worst imagined scenario, they'd disown me, never wanting to see me again.

When I told them, my mom screamed repeatedly, "No daughter of mine." She said she should've had me married straight out of college and begged me not to tell a soul of what she considered to be my "sickness." Although her words were painful, I wasn't surprised by them. My dad's response, however, was totally unexpected.

I spent much of my life constantly being judged by my dad, and it always seemed like he regarded me with disappointment. When I revealed my sexual identity to him, he seemed angry. He asked, "How long? How long have you known this about yourself?" I told him that I knew I was different as early as eighteen, and then braced myself for his ire. After all, I had been lying to my dad for the better part of my adult life. However, he said with a hurting heaviness, "What kind of father am I that my own daughter couldn't trust me enough to tell me such a thing for all these years." The floodgates to something quite beautiful and powerful flew open, and the wall, which I'd spent years carefully erecting, began to disintegrate.

Later that evening, when things with my mom finally settled down, he and I talked for hours, which was the longest I'd ever talked to my dad at one time. He wanted to know what he could do differently and where he went wrong. He listened to me and was really open to feedback. For the first time in my life, I experienced him as someone who wanted to learn about and grow closer to me. That night, my dad showed me the depth of his love for and acceptance of me, and I was stunned by it. Since then, he and I've worked to rebuild our relationship and he's become a different kind of father.

Also, after years of keeping my sexuality a secret from my extended family at the behest of my mother, I came out to them as well. They didn't blink an eye and treated me with warmth and loving-kindness. I assume they could feel all the energy I'd put into hiding and were waiting for me with open arms when I finally came out.

Through it all, I have her, my now wife, to thank for these marvelous shifts of life. In a roundabout, karmic kind of way, she gave me my dad. She gave me my family. And all she did was to be herself which provided a roadmap to my own limitlessness. I am beyond thankful that our paths united once again.

As for my mom, she's slowly but surely coming around.

Based on VS's story

My Complicated Relationship

My relationship with my mother
Is complicated.

I accept it.
She doesn't get me.
I don't entirely get her.

We find each other maddening
At times. She pushes.
I pull. She pulls.
I shove her away. We cycle
Through lows and highs,
As she experiences downs and ups.

But she and I belong to each other.

For so long, we were all we had.
When food was scarce, and candles were lit
To stretch our dollars long—when thirty-day
Eviction notices graced our front door,
And medical bills piled high—when simple pleasures
Were precious luxuries, and we dressed in thirdhand fineries
To sit in the back row of the ballet—

We were all we had.

Based on AG's story

My Scattered Pieces

I fight away her darkness
Which attempts to ingrain itself within my psyche.
Loneliness terrorizes the corners of my mind,
Making it so I can't sleep in silence.
At times, I feel unsettled in the wholeness of my body.

Long ago, she banished pieces of me to her shadowlands,
Refusing to hold me as it would cause her to break down
    in tears.
I reminded her too much of my father
Who she longed for and hated.
He abandoned her a year and a half into my existence
Which is a weight upon my chest I carry, although I crave
    liberation.
She once told me they never wanted another child,
But I arrived anyway, innocent and fragile.

Early childhood memories etched melancholy into my
    awareness.
When I was a little girl, not even three feet tall,
I'd stand in her doorway, hoping she'd collect me in her arms
And gently rock me to sleep.
A piece of me remains there, still.
In vain, I'd go from room to room and turn on all the lights,
Silently pleading for her to notice me.
She never did no matter how I tried.

Before bed, I'd lock all the doors and windows
Because I didn't feel safe in the pit of my gut or marrow of
    my bones.

Despite those precautions, I'd lie awake in bed waiting for
   the worst.
Worry tainted the prettiest of thoughts—
Of being severely hurt, stolen away, or consumed in a fire—

Who could save a little girl who couldn't be seen?

A long, winding road led from my house to a beautiful beach.
I'd walk there and play for hours in the sand,
Asking myself all the while,
"Does she notice I'm gone?
Will she ever hold me?
Will she ever see me?"
A piece of me remains there,
Building castles to be carried away
By laps of water along the shore.

Based on Wendy's story

Happy Birthday, Dad. I Love You

(Dedicated to Darryl Davis)

Happy birthday, dearest Dad,
From your one and only little girl.
I miss you so, so much
And often relive the memories
Between us that never were.
I shed a million and one tears
Each year on this special day,
Because my heart breaks
When it remembers
You aren't here with me.

I used to imagine you walking through the front door
In an incredible surprise,
Because the Fates brought you back to life,
Correcting their misguided mistake
Of ushering your spirit away too soon.

And then you'd kiss me
Lovingly on my forehead,
Wipe the tears from my eyes,
And hold me very, very tight,
Never letting me go.
I'd lay my head upon your chest,
Listen to your heartbeat, and sigh
Because you'd finally returned home.

While I've put that dream to rest,
I'll never not wish for your presence.
I love you, Dad.

Happy Birthday,
Happy Birthday,
Happy Birthday to you.

Based on the story of Anonymous

To My Sister: When I Was Three and You Were Five

Sister, remember when I was three
And you were five?
I loved it when we played together
On those too hot summer days,
Running through the sprinklers,
Hide and seek,
Noisily eating cherry red popsicles
That dripped lazily onto the sidewalk.
The lemonade stand
We thought would make us millionaires.
I can see us in a yesterday
That was so long ago.

Since then, I've missed you.
I mean really, truly missed you.
But we grew up, and for so long
I missed you.

You were on the receiving end
Of my too hot to touch anger.
When you tried to be there for me,
I lashed out, and you were burned.
The anger was so big, I had to give it to someone.

I should've seen how badly you were hurting
As your words became covered with ice.
You'd always say, "Leave me alone,"
And so I left you.
Alone.

Sister, please know, I was hurting too.
Is that a poor excuse
For why I wasn't always there for you?

If I saw through your words to the very truth of you,
I'd have recognized a part of myself and known your pain
Was so big, you had to give it to someone.

Sister, remember when I was three
And you were five?
Oh, that was such an untroubled time.
If I could go back to my littler self,
I'd whisper in her ear and say,
There'll be times when she hurts you.
Forgive her.
There'll be times when she ignores you.
Be there for her anyway.
There'll be times when you want to call her out of her name.
Bite your tongue.
There'll be times when you want to shut her out.
Embrace her.
There'll be times when she says she hates you.
Love her.
Life won't ever be as easy as it is right now.
You'll need each other to get through it.

Based on Britteney Bass's story

My Ride with Grandpa

The sky reflects a moody blue-grey.
I roll all the windows down
So that my hair billows with the breeze.
Fall scenes whir by in brilliant strokes
Of orange, red and gold. I listen
To the engine for when to change gears
As I mount the open road
With knowing command.

I'm transported through reverie
To vivid memories of the car
He rebuilt bit by bit
After waiting countless hours in line
To obtain the exact right parts.
He loved to drive back country roads
For hours upon hours in that car.

A humble rush of wind brings
Me the vibrance of his glow,
Great in its love and intensity,
Sitting in the passenger's seat.

Could it be?
Is it you that I feel with me?
It is! It is!
There's so much, so much to say!
Where should I begin?

I named my son after you
So he would possess your strength

Which moved mountains.
He's already like you in so many ways.
There are instants when I catch myself
Watching him, captivated,
Because I see you.
If only he could've experienced
Your encompassing and unyielding protection.
But he cherishes you.
I make sure of that.

And Grandma.
Ah! There hasn't ever been a day, after all these years,
That she doesn't think of you,
Even when she smiles, it's written all over her face—
The pain of her longing for your smile and touch.
It's like part of her light dimmed
The very second you departed.
Although you and I don't believe in God,
I pray to experience the soul-rocking,
Earth-making, transcendent
Kind of love that you two shared.
It may hurt like hell one day,
But the love will make it all worth it.

I am quiet for several minutes
And then several minutes more
As tears began to gather in my eyes.

When you passed away, I couldn't cry.
Mom never understood why.
But the thought of never seeing you
Or hearing your voice again
Was too much for me to bear.
I couldn't shed a single tear,

Although I mourned you in my own way.
I hoped you knew I had changed
And was no longer in the throes
Of a critically turbulent phase.
I didn't want your last thoughts of me
To be tainted by my dark moods.
Yet as I feel you with me now,
I am reminded that you knew me
Before I ever knew myself
And loved me regardless
Of the things I did or said.

After being lost in the vastness of that rustic road,
I realize I've returned home, and it's time for him to go.

I turn off the engine and whisper . . .

There's much more I want to say.
Please, come back.
Come back to me one day.

Based on Sasha Zolley's story

Why I Didn't Buy Pads Until I Was Twenty-One

I don't recall getting my first period. I don't remember the day or what I was wearing. It wasn't some special event where my mom threw me a period party with a banner that read "WELCOME TO WOMANHOOD," or anything like that. I know I was in the sixth grade and elated that the red stain in my panties graduated me to shop in the junior's section of JC Penny. I was also horrified that the big, boxy pads of the time made having a period a hard secret to keep. My parents prepared me to grow up, and I read everything about growing up, so at twelve years old, getting a period was a natural part of life. It meant that I'd have to shower more, would get cramps monthly, was getting older, and could have a baby.

What stands out to me most is that, for a long while, my dad consistently bought the women of the house pads and chocolate every time he went to Costco. In fact, I didn't buy pads until I was twenty-one. Stereotypes depict men as being confused and embarrassed about buying feminine products for their wives, girlfriends, and daughters, but that wasn't my dad. He had no shame in plopping several packs of winged Kotex into his grocery cart.

My dad was the provider, as were the men before him. My mom took good care of us and the upkeep of our home which was a lot of work, and my dad made sure she had what she needed to do so. In many ways, it was very traditional. She didn't have to punch into a nine to five or even learn to drive. My dad covered the costs of bills and incidentals and took us wherever we wanted to go. My mom also never had to take out the trash, mow the lawn, or fix major issues around the house. She most definitely never ever bought pads.

Looking back, I am thankful that my dad was such a provider, although it had its drawbacks. For instance, he always got the big piece of chicken, however, after all he did for us, it makes sense. Also, he wasn't very big on emotion and was disinclined to have serious heart-to-hearts. We never talked about me getting my period in the sixth grade. The closest mention of Aunt Flo came one day when he said, "I read that chocolate has nothing to do with that time of the month, so I am going to stop buying it and don't go asking for it." After that, he just bought pads. Ultimately, he didn't make any real effort to understand me. I wonder if, in his mind, he didn't have to if I had what was essential to be successful in life. I'm glad he was there for us in his way.

When I was a kid, I thought it was so gross when I'd hear adults say, "girls want to marry their fathers." It was such a confusing and odd statement to wrap my head around—girls marrying their fathers. I understand perfectly now. When my time comes, I want my life partner to be a provider and someone who prioritizes my needs. If a man ever says to me, "well what about my needs?" I'd know he wasn't the one. That's because a provider is aware that if he takes care of his partner, she can take care of the world which includes him in it. Does that mean I want to be a traditional stay at home wife/mom? Not necessarily, although I haven't ruled it out as a possibility. It means that I want a man who can confidently stroll down a store's feminine care aisle and get the exact right thing. I want him to get the chocolate, too. So what if it has nothing to do with my period?

Based on the story of Anonymous

She Carried Me. I Carried Her.

Intuitively in touch with her agony,
I sensed she was ailing, immediately reversing course
To return home, forgetting about the errand
Which made me leave in a single-minded hurry.

I found her fallen from her motorized chair,
Severely twisted on the ground.
The hot summer sun reddened her skin,
Showing she'd lain there half an hour or more.
As I swiftly ran to her side,
Panic quickened my breath.

Every bone in her body
Was bent askew.
I collected her carefully in my arms
And sighed a prayer of gratitude
That she was only bruised.

She was so determined
To fight for vigor and vitality
Against the will of her disease.
Why else would she have ventured outdoors
Without the protection of friend or family?

When I was a child, she did all the protecting.
She shielded me from unseen monsters
When I wasn't aware
And raised me with attentive care.
She soothed my cries,
Cleaned every one of my sniffly noses,

Bandaged my cuts and scrapes to good as new,
And kissed the hurt from every owie and boo-boo.

Then, she got sick, and our roles changed.
Blessedly her love contained a wellspring of strength
Which I drew from when I was tired and drained
To carry her as she once carried me.

Based on the story of Anonymous

My Family's Dinner Table

I anticipate each movement
Amid persistent misery
At my family's dinner table.

Unfailingly,
I laugh and smile
Past the point of my heart's ache
To bring momentary peace
And interrupt their resolve
To break hell loose
With the might of muted rage.

Laughter quells the disquieted,
And broad smiles briefly dissipate
Melancholy hanging about the air,
Gifting time for captured breaths
To find their respite.

All the while, I teeter
At the edge of a crack,
Silently praying to be saved.

Based on the story of Anonymous

I Choose Them That Call Me Mommy

None of the things I've accomplished in this life measure up to how proud I am of my children. Being their mom is a uniquely special adventure. I love them more than I thought I could ever love anyone or anything. In fact, had I not become a mom, I would've never fathomed my ability to love so much and so deeply. Still, I struggle almost every day and, prior to having my first child, doubted whether motherhood was for me.

Having children was my husband's choice. To him, it was part of the natural course of things—get married, buy a house, have kids. I, conversely, would've been fine with—get married, buy a house, wake up late on Saturday mornings, from time to time eat an entire jar of Nutella in bed. In my early to mid-twenties, I can't say I factored children into my original equation for adulthood. Growing up and determining the course of my life was already a huge undertaking. I wasn't sure what to do, where to go, or who to be. But then I met my husband who seemed to have things figured out.

Soon after we got married, he said, "Let's have a baby."
I said, "Okay."
Nine months later, my first child was born.
Two years after that he said, "Let's have another kid," and I said, "Okay."
Nine months later, our second child came. In the midst of baby making, I put self-discovery on hold.

I'm amazed that these remarkable little people I co-created and who grow more and more each day call me Mommy.

Being their mommy feels so good . . . and so nerve-wracking. I imagine that every wrong thing I do will F-up their lives forever. A friend told me there isn't such a thing as perfect parenting, only *good enough*. I want to believe that, I really do, but there are so many days when I feel like I'm getting a big, fat F in the Mommy Department. Like when they're tired and cranky because I let them stay up too late. FAIL. Or when they're jittery because I let them have too much sugar. FAIL. Or when I snap at them because I'm overwhelmed. FAIL. Or when I send store-bought, instead of homemade, cupcakes for school bake sales. FAIL. If I were successful, everyone would be happy and healthy, the house would be consistently clean, and there'd be a nutritious dinner prepared on time each night. I also wouldn't be stressed out all the time about being behind in everything.

Looking back, those first couple of years of motherhood were a fight. I fought against the fundamental day to day changes of life. I fought against losing my sense of self, which was already in flux before I became a mom. I fought against my time no longer being mine. When I gave birth to my first child, my life instantly shifted to keeping this tiny being alive. That shift was a hard one, to say the least.

Fortunately, things started to get easier after our second child was born. I began to really appreciate that no matter how much my identity changes, *Mom* will always be part of it, and what I give them is different from what anyone else can give them. Also, I love being a witness to who they are becoming and am honored that I get to be their mom. So, although I regularly feel insecure about my mothering abilities and find motherhood generally challenging, I choose my children. I always will, even though I didn't definitively choose this life.

Based on A's story

My First Memory

Unbridled fits of laughter
At a greater-than-life legend
Adorned in a white doctor's coat
Dancing in the spotlight
On our living room's stage,
My brother's tighty-whities
Gracing the top of his head
As his bright cloth crown.

I clap with admiration and glee,
In sync with every *haw haw* and *hee hee*,
As his most ardent fan.

I implore for encore after encore,
So he repeatedly twirls and leaps
In pirouettes across the floor
With such pronounced seriousness
That I giggle all the more.

Based on the story of Anonymous

His Crumpled Socks

Dad settling in to watch TV after work—
Peeling them off from heel to toe
And leaving them on the living room floor . . .
Again.

Mom getting mad,
The last straw being had,
Breaking our home into two.

I closed my eyes for a second,
Opened them,
And he was gone
For good this time.

Remnants of him
Were here and there.
Family pictures.
His favorite chair.

The house was quieter.
Emptier.

When no one was looking,
I'd cry and cry and cry and cry
Almost every day for a good long while.

Tears gave way to rage and recklessness.
I had control over nothing
And wanted to fight everyone.

I spoke to a counselor a few times. He asked,
"What do you think caused their divorce?"

I shrugged and replied,

"His crumpled socks."

Based on Britteney Bass's story

Thank You, Mom. Love, Me.

Thank you
For keeping us safe
And cooking us fresh meals
After your long days.
Thank you
For gifting me
With a childhood
Absent of the trials
Of growing up too fast.
Thank you
For the consistency of your presence,
Steady, true, and comforting.

I couldn't see the contemplation behind your decisions
Or the many parts of life you juggled with a single hand,
And I was upset with you for working against my anti-
    system values.

Now I see
You did the best
With what you were given.
I'm all the better for it.
Thank you
For my life.
Love, me.

Based on the story of Anonymous

My Family Lines

The lines on my hands tell the stories
Of my mothers and fathers across lifetimes and generations.
My existence, cast from their blood and bones,
Was shaped by their collective hardships and joys.
I'm a living realization of their decisions . . .

To leap into Atlantic waters and swim to the shore
Of a new land, overflowing with opportunities.
To run away on bare feet from a winter's hawk that robbed
Cupboards and stomachs bare.
To work endless nights and long days.

To relinquish two small children to a young and worried
    husband
When the walls of mind fractured.
To move out at just eighteen to marry a first love,
Despite a disapproving family swearing to *never accept him.*
To keep silent and avoid the pain of words.

To push forward after returning home from a thankless war
Where friends were made and then lost.
To care for a father and younger brother while a grief-
    stricken mother
Mourned for an eldest daughter taken suddenly.
To live against all odds.

The lines on my hands tell their stories.

Based on the story of Anonymous

. . . in my joy, magic, strength, and possibilities

My Joyous Return

From the plane, just below the clouds,
Distinct and lustrous mountain tops
Manifest from childhood dreams
Into an adult reality.

Descent elicits awe and reverence
For the misty veils,
Gently covering green, green trees
And the islands and the sea—
A paradise on earth.

After years of suffering constant constraint,
My breath releases in great exhalation.
With it comes tears of unmitigated relief
Which wash away the stagnant well
Of what I've left behind.

I take in a pure, exalted breath
And then another and another,
Until new air circulates
Within and around me.

A previously inaccessible future
Begins to grow within my mind's eye.
My spirit rises in joyful ascension.
Although this place is completely
New to me, I've finally returned home.

Based on VS's story

The Last Vestige of My Youth

One day, I'm going to put my little girl in the car, and we'll go for a drive to a peaceful place. Maybe to the park where I can push her on the swings, or to a nice green picnic area by the water. The past will forever be in the rearview mirror as we look forward to what's to come. I have to get my driver's license, though.

At sixteen, I attempted, with no luck, to crossover that teenaged rite. I took a driver's ed class but dropped out of high school in the middle of the course. My mom tried to teach me, but I was too nervous to learn anything. I'd constantly brake three feet before a stop sign or start making turns early. I was so bad that eventually, no one wanted to teach me.

I resolved to have older friends and boyfriends who could drive me around. I also hitchhiked, which is something I'll never advise my daughter to do. Eventually, I moved to a place with an abundance of public transportation. Learning to drive became the very last thing on my mind. It's since become the last thing holding me back as a vestige of a time gone by.

Growing up, I was so different from my peers. I experienced a profound depression in high school which made connecting with other kids my age challenging. It didn't help that my family got by on a very limited income. Based on my appearance, it was obvious I was poor, and in high school, that alone classified me as a social outcast. With a white mom and black dad, I was racially different, too. Very few people looked like me or shared in my racial identity.

When I dropped out and obtained my GED, it took me some time to enter college. While others had graduated and were preparing to enter the workforce, I was a newly minted freshman. I graduated when people my age were already established in their careers. It was as if my entire twenties were spent being in a different stage of life compared to everyone else. I was still an outsider.

Years later, I am settled in my career, and have a wonderful husband and beautiful daughter. I am thankful to all my experiences for getting me here, and immensely proud of myself for all I've accomplished. It's no small feat to graduate from college as a high school dropout. It's no easy task to keep pressing forward when it's easier to give up. But still, I can't drive. I am determined to learn, though. I want to take my daughter everywhere.

Based on Kelsey Norton's story

When Music Takes It's Hold of Me: Thank You, Tracy Chapman

Her song on the radio
Reaches for me,
Taking hold of my spirit
As a blissful remedy
For the anxieties of my mind.
I give in, initially with a small sway,
As I let her carry me away—
A multicolored kite
Finding its escape
On the back of a rippling gale,

Eyes close to journey
Along the path of harmony,
Lips move silently with the words,
Until I discover
The lyrics of my voice
And let out a guttural,
Commanding howl—
An infant birthed
From the womb.

Senses are tuned
By vibrations,
Swaying becomes dance,
Feet tap in remembrance.

I'm at home
In the organic movements

Of my body, without worry
Of occupying
Too much or too little space.

I transform into an expansive oak tree
Then contract into a droplet of rain.

No matter my size,
I'm gingerly held between
Each breath and beat.
I don't think, *I'm not enough.*

Based on Wendy's story

The Twilight of My Vision

When darkness falls,
The margins disappear.
I transition in perception
While moving through a tunnel
Of floating lights and
Everyday silhouettes.

It's the kind of rare affliction
That makes a broken streetlight
Turn the earth on its axis
For a disorienting second or two.
I make sure to get home in one piece,
None the worse for wear.

Some might say I'm distant
In the face of their concerns
Because I conceal my insecurities
Behind a fortress of self-reliance.
But I'm learning to trust my loved ones
To handle my vulnerabilities with care
As I knock down my walls
One solid piece at a time.

Independence
Is my trusted passport
To depart the panic and trepidation
Languishing in the far reaches of my mind.
In lieu of worrying,

I prefer to savor opalescent sunsets
Giving way to the twilight of my vision.

Based on the story of Anonymous

The Still, Small Voice Inside of Me

*When a hiker embarks on a worthwhile
journey and follows the path before her, she
will reap her intended blessings, even when she
doesn't know where the path will take her.*

I woke up one morning with a still, small voice inside of me
saying, "You need to buy a plane ticket to Jackson, Mississippi."
I responded with, "Who's going with me? Am I to do this
alone?" So, I decided to sit with the thought in the days that
followed and see if it would resonate. Admittedly, I was scared
to embark on such an unknown journey and didn't initially
trust the voice that encouraged me to do something so out of
my comfort zone. However, when I revisited that voice and
asked it if I was meant to travel to Jackson, the resounding
answer was, "YES!" I purchased my ticket immediately.

I'd never traveled to Mississippi, yet was very connected
to it as the home of my paternal forebears where my kindred
bloodlines run deep into the land. I discovered this while
doing ancestral research on my father's side of the family,
healing work that helped me to process my grief over his
loss. Buying that ticket was like stepping onto a path to
find a part of myself that was lost. I had no idea why I was
going or what to look for. I only knew I had to listen. And
so, one Memorial Day, I took a plane to Jackson.

I set foot on Mississippi soil with a long drive ahead
of me, and a few addresses and documents in hand, not
knowing where to begin. I connected to that still, small
voice and messages popped into my head. The first said to
visit the house my late grandfather built in a town outside

of the city. Going there spurred my memory to recall the time when my father sent flowers to his maternal aunt's memorial service which was held at a school nearby.

I drove to the school and was led to a literal dead end. I saw a man standing next to his truck as if he were waiting for someone. Something told me to ask him about nearby cemeteries. "You lookin' for the black one, or the white one?" he asked. I was excited and gob smacked all at once and asked for directions to the black cemetery.

I found the cemetery in half well-maintained, half unkempt condition. I was guided to walk the aisles of the latter and spent at least ninety minutes searching for my family. Most of the headstones were broken, and weeds covered much of the ground, making names unrecognizable. As I was about to explore other parts of the graveyard, I looked down and saw my great auntie's name in clear engraved letters. I fell to my knees and started to cry as chills surged down my spine. I instantly knew her spirit was with me and became filled with immense gratitude.

It turns out there are many black cemeteries in that area, but I was sent to that one. It wasn't by chance. It was her connecting with me, me connecting with her, and the Creator leading me to that moment. The Holy Spirit— that still, small voice—was guiding me to her, and to the realization that my ancestors are with me and wanting acknowledgement.

The trip to Mississippi was when I followed the path as it was shown, without looking for answers to the left or right. Instead, I stayed the course with faith in my heart and was rewarded with life-changing revelations. I was also reminded that when I stop thinking and start trusting, life works very well. What true blessings indeed!

Based on the story of Anonymous

My Plunge into Freedom

Jump! Jump! Jump!
Their cheers were overwhelming.
I eventually tuned them out
And could only hear
My booming thoughts.

The clear blue water delicately
Flowed into a far off forever.
It was getting late.
The sun was soon to set beneath the sky.
I would miss my chance.

Everyone else already had a turn.
I stood there alone, shaking uncontrollably.

I remembered
The support
Of the rocks underfoot.

They held me steady
When I thought I'd crumble.
I'm not afraid of heights,
But I was terrified.
I'd never jumped without a net.

My heart beat loudly within my ears
As I negotiated fate with myself.
"Don't do it," I said, "The risk is too great."
"But everyone else did it," I replied,
"Nothing happened to them.

Why should I be the one to miss out
Because I'm scared!"

Before I grasped my feet were no longer planted,
I was leaping high into the air
And free falling until water rushed over my head.

I swam to the surface,
Beaming with lightness.
Triumphant.

Based on the story of Anonymous

An Important Lesson My Dad Taught Me

"Dad, help me. I'm stuck!"

It was dark, wet, and muddy, and I was terrified, thinking I might drown. I kept my little face held towards the sky as I cried out. At three years old, I hadn't yet learned how to swim. I had fallen into a sinkhole next to the riverbank, and my dad peered down at me and said, "No, you're not going to drown, and you're not stuck. What you're going to do is stand up and walk out of that sinkhole all by yourself."

People might think that my dad took quite the unsympathetic stance to my circumstance. I was a small child, after all. But maybe there was a part of him that wanted me to learn about the power of choice. I could've cried and remained stuck in fear, waiting for him to give in, or learned how to save myself, which is exactly what I did. I dug myself free from the darkness, and the mud, and the wetness. That experience was formative and defining. Life is, after all, full of sinkholes.

When I encounter them, I don't sit around expecting someone to swoop in and save the day, although there are instances when I'm thoroughly overwhelmed and want to be rescued. I'm, ultimately, my own superhero whose primary power is the ability to do anything I set my mind to do, because I can't rely on others to do things for me. I've been through many challenging and seemingly hopeless situations; however, I consistently make choices to move forward, never failing or giving up. Otherwise, I'd be trembling in the dark, still stuck. Waiting.

Based on the story of Anonymous

Changing My Narrative

Loveable in every way,
I keep lurking doubts at bay;

Their sharp hooks
Strike at hard-earned confidence.

If I let them latch
Onto bumped and shiny wounds

They'd lure me into making myself relevant
To those unmindful of my beauty.

Based on Van Nguyen's story

The Time I Was Reborn in the Northern Mountains

As a young girl, I was too frightened to walk to school alone, but I had to once a week. Without fail, on the eve of this day, I'd quake with dread in my bed, unable to fall asleep. At the time, my relationship to my body was tenuous, and I was weak from regular starvation. In my mind, anything could happen to me on that walk, because I was defenseless and physically unable to protect myself. Somehow, it was more important to be safe than strong, as almost everything in life made me scared. However, during that walk to school, I didn't feel safe or strong.

After years of fear dictating my life, I was reborn.

It happened one summer while I was in college. All my friends were graduating and moving on to whatever immediate future awaited them. I, to the contrary, took a semester off in rebellion against the status quo of the professional rat race. The idea of submitting hundreds of resumes, going on dozens of interviews, giving canned answers to nameless HR reps to ultimately get a job I'd hate was demoralizing and devaluing. It seemed the world was telling me my worth was tied to what I did for a living and how much money I made without regard for my identity. I was sick and tired of being implicitly told what I had to look like and who I had to be. Instead of getting a summer job before my last semester, I drained my savings and went on a long hike into the spacious unknown.

I began the expedition with a friend—someone who's status in my life was, "it's complicated." We drove from school to the northern mountains before I decided I no longer wanted him as my traveling companion. I hoisted my bag on my shoulders and stood alone, strong, and powerful, as I watched him drive away. I spent the entire summer by myself, trekking through the mountains in self-loving defiance of society's rigid norms. I carried everything I needed on my back and never worried about having too much or too little.

I hiked under the sun's hot rays and during torrid rains with the earth as my home and confidant. There was no place to hide from the simple complexities of nature which was inspiring and humbling. My own nature emerged, freed from the fear of existing. I made every decision for myself and determined my own pace. I learned to follow the signs by listening to my intuition, and experienced indescribable magic as a result.

What's more, a large part of my youth was spent in disembodiment. My body was a thing to be controlled and manipulated to fit manmade standards. I taught myself to ignore its signals when I was hungry, tired, and depleted. That summer, I was completely in my body, and allowed it to resurrect one movement at a time. I paid attention to what it needed, how it felt, and what it asked of me. I met extraordinary people along the way and developed spiritually intimate relationships with them where I often showed up unshowered, and dirty from the hike. That didn't matter to them or me. I was truly present with them in intense and beautiful ways, and my body was able to feel what it was formerly deprived of.

I re-emerged transformed by my journey. I began to make choices that others wouldn't based on what's right for me, not on what society implicitly or explicitly tells me to do. This includes how I nourish my body, where I live, who I'm friends with, who I choose as a partner, what I do for work, when I work, and how much I get paid. Essentially, I treat my life like a hike through the mountains where I am directed by the truth of my innermost compass.

Based on the story of Anonymous

I Love Myself Unapologetically

Those who abide by their insecurities
Want to drag me into a pit
Of self-loathing.
I nonchalantly resist
And am hated by them for it.
To be honest,
I don't care if they hate me.

I love myself
Unapologetically.
I am too talented,
Too gifted,
Too prepared
To succumb to a lesser life.
I'll always choose myself
Over being liked
By crabs in a barrel.

I love myself
With all my heart and soul,
So I follow through
To fulfil my dreams,
Working backwards
Through every detail
Until delicious fruit ripens
Into sweet opportunities.
When I don't succeed,
I own my failures,
Because I know my value
Will remain undiminished.

And I adore
The tone of my brown complexion
Which glows from the inside out.
My bottom lip is a rich
Pink, contrasting
With the cinnamon hue
Of the top one.
My eyes are dark, liquid brown.
When I look in the mirror,
I can't help but lovingly stare
At the one staring back at me.

Some rebuke my confidence
With pleasure
And throw ugly epithets
At my frame.

What of it?
I love myself,
And will always be beautiful to me.

Based on the story of Anonymous

Itchy Feet and My Escape from the Expected

I got my sense of adventure and curiosity from my mom. Although she was never able to prioritize globe trekking as she wanted, she traveled in her mind and spirit, frequently taking me with her. As a child, my youth was spent visiting all sorts of museums, going to concerts which featured artists from around the world, and attending plays that revealed the human experience. My mom also made sure that I grew up around tons of books which transported me to fantastical places. Therefore, it wasn't shocking to her when, as a senior in college, I decided to take a semester off to live in France.

By the time senior year arrived, I was in a state of perpetual ennui. School became stifling and suffocating to my soul. I knew I wasn't going to graduate in the spring, and my feet began to itch terribly. I didn't just want to break free from the doldrums. It was imperative. I started by taking trips around the country, visiting places I'd never been. My family never took vacations or road trips together, so hopping on a plane or taking off by car to visit another part of my fifty-state backyard was eye-opening. I wanted to see more.

A good friend of mine always talked about her overseas adventures which were quite extensive, piquing my interest. I yearned to have similar experiences. I couldn't travel abroad my junior year, as I hadn't positioned myself academically to do so; yet I knew senior year was my opportunity to do something different. While my friends were preparing to graduate that spring, I was researching ways to postpone graduation to live abroad.

Although my parents weren't surprised by my decision, they were initially hesitant to offer support. They were afraid that if I left school, I wouldn't go back—a valid fear at the time. Yet they knew I couldn't stay where I was. My parents said that if I found a program where I could study, they would help me financially, but I'd have to pay for my last semester of school when I returned to the US. I agreed, knowing I just had to get out.

I found a program in Paris that worked out perfectly with my finances and schedule. Once I exited Charles de Gaulle Airport, I smelled the air around me and was exhilarated, unbound, and free. I lived in a small room over an alley which was an ideal space to lay my head, as I spent much of my time exploring the places I'd read about and having fun with new friends. The architecture, the art, the history, the culture, the people—my cup was full every single day.

When I came home, I carried my sense of freedom with me, and gave myself permission to NOT figure out what I was supposed to do with my life. I didn't know and didn't have to know. I focused on what I wanted to do in the here and now which entailed exploring my city, going to book readings, seeing interesting films, hanging out with friends, and meeting people. I gave little thought to working behind a desk for eight hours a day or going to grad school which previously seemed like the only two options I had after college.

I also waitressed during my last semester, saving up enough money to pay off the remainder of my undergraduate debt, and resume my travels. My dream was to work in sub-Saharan Africa. I came upon a position which required me to train in Denmark for six weeks before going to the motherland. I went back to France to visit friends before embarking on a new adventure. My plans shifted day by day, and I never made it to Denmark. However, I spent the next six months in Europe living fully, openly, and courageously. Although I continue to dream vividly of Africa, I've no regrets and will one day inhale its vibrant energy. Life unfolded exactly the way it needed to.

__Based on D's story__

My Life's Mission in Three Parts

To be a vessel
For reconciliation
Truth and honesty

To set the space
For healing fear with compassion
And humility

To facilitate
A thorough dismantling
Of white supremacy

Based on the story of Anonymous

Forging a Path Laid by My Dad's Footsteps

I burst into tears during lunch. I didn't want to and was immediately self-conscious, thinking everyone in the restaurant was staring at me. I couldn't stop the hiccupping sobs that developed into what some might call an ugly cry. I was out with my family, celebrating my graduation from grad school, when my dad handed me the small white envelope that induced the waterworks. I opened it, not knowing what to expect, and my hands flew to my mouth in surprise.

A check for $1,000! Honestly, it wasn't the money that sparked my powerful emotion. It was receiving my dad's acknowledgement. He worked hard his whole life, ever since he was a kid, for every single cent. Throughout his life, he fought for survival. Nothing, absolutely nothing, was handed to him. Receiving that check, which I know he busted his butt for, was him tipping his hat to me for my perseverance and hard-earned accomplishments.

When I initially entered grad school for social work, I shamefully dropped out after three weeks. It was overwhelming and different from undergrad. But, as the saying goes, "if at first you don't succeed, try, try, try again," and try again I did. I was determined to go back and finish something that was on my heart to do. When I went back to school, I was working fulltime, and rather than quit my job, I decided to attend as an evening student so I could do both. The grad school program also required that I complete a sixteen hour a week internship each semester and during the summers. My plate was constantly overflowing with busyness.

For three years of my life, I somehow managed to balance all these obligations. In the beginning, I wasn't sure if or how I'd finish. I pushed through sleepless nights to write papers and study for exams, only to then wake up early for work. It was demanding, to say the least. Fortunately, I eventually found a nice rhythm to my life. What especially got me through was genuine excitement to learn of different ways of looking at problems and their solutions. I tried to absorb every piece of information I could with the hopes of changing the world through service to community.

Those years were challenging, but I successfully made it to the other side of them. Through it all, I dreamed of making my dad proud and showing him, I was able to succeed because he made the way. In the end, he really saw me working hard to get to a better place and live life with purpose. That moment at lunch was the pinnacle of my dream come true.

Based on the story of Anonymous

My Winding Nature

My nature buds and blooms
Against the rooted wall,
Organically, freely,
As if touched by Earth's
Knobbed and gnarly hands
In benediction.

It's to allow the unfurling
Of my vines
To flow with the melodies
Of Wind, Sun, and Rain
While bowing to the blossoming flowers
And rising trees
In loving acknowledgement.

That is my nature.

It is neither this nor that.
I find solace in its
Meek and undefined passivity.

Based on the story of Anonymous

My Last Ballet Class

I tugged hard on my leotard, uncomfortable with the way it made me feel. Restricted somehow. Maybe it was because I hated pink, or that I didn't enjoy ballet, although it seemed every girl at that age was doing it. Pliéing, relevéing, leaping, twirling. There's nothing wrong with ballet, but it just wasn't me.

As I practiced delicate movements, I recalled the priest at school who called me a feminist. I vehemently disagreed with his opinion that a nun couldn't emulate Jesus. I couldn't see why not and gave him a sound argument about why I was right. He made me do pushups, and then labeled me a feminist as if it were a four-letter word. I think he imagined he'd pinned some sort of Scarlet F on my chest that day. But, instead of being ashamed, I wore it with prideful resistance to the invisible hand trying to fit me into its mold of institutionalization.

I spun awkwardly across the floor to the sound of classical music, and I thought to myself, *not every girl wants to point her toes with precision or wear a cotton candy tutu. Some of us want to boom and stomp and skat, and HA!* I decided that would be my last day at practicing ballet. I wanted to make loud sounds that can only come from metal soled shoes brushing and clicking against the floor.

Based on A's story

My Beauty Belongs to Me

I can't dispute
The completeness of my
Beauty. I admire a dark
Complexion confidently
Glittering in the noonday sun.

My beauty belongs to me.

I know the truth
Of its existence was birthed
In my loving and unrepentant gaze.

Yet as I roam the contours
And curves of its delicate shape,
I feel a strange and painful
Dissonance that intends
To unground me
From the power in which I stand—

Dissonance made manifest
By a procession of lower beings
Who create a cacophony
Of debased desire to possess
What is not theirs to own.

They fashion tiny portals
Through concrete to spy on
My naked form, endeavor to enter
Private places without permission,
And attempt to brand me with their wanton words.

I fight to remain firmly planted
While holding my beauty
Safely in my mind's eye.

I dispute their entitlement.
I am not
Their honey-baby.
I am not
Their submissive concubine.
I am not
The personification of their trauma.
I am
Mine.

Based on SC's story

. . . in my healing

My Healing Is

My healing is messy, chaotic, and confusing.
It's magnificent and full of sheer joy and playfulness.
It's giving attention to my unsettled parts.

My healing is reflecting, sitting, and unpacking while
   remembering nothing is insurmountable.
It's the space where my emotions can feel instead of
   rationalize.
It welcomes vulnerability.

My healing is filling my days with what I look forward to
And protecting my peace from the chatter of my mind.
It's not letting my pain fundamentally affect who I am.

It's really moving forward, no matter how long it takes.
It's really moving forward, no matter how long it takes.
It's really moving forward, no matter how long it takes.

My healing is about releasing, evolving, and integrating.
It's about engaging, overcoming, recovering, and repairing.
It's seeing the possibilities in every grain of sand as ocean
   waves bring coolness to my feet.

My healing is screaming into a pillow after a long day to
   find my inner calm.
It's being patient enough to change what I can without
   expecting to be made whole
And allowing myself to love and be loved without hiding
   from my truth.

My healing means putting the right label on what I'm feeling.
It's unwinding what is inside of me so that I can forgive myself
And making amends so that I can forgive others.

It lives in letting go.
It lives in letting go.
It lives in letting go.

My healing lies within the freedom of my expression.
It's running, cooking, dancing, gardening, singing, and
   painting.
It's collaging, sculpting, journaling, and *talking it through*.

My healing is shifting my perspective and trusting my
   intuition.
It's seeing the beauty of my scars left after cutting
   emotional cords
And in knowing what I do and don't deserve and what is
   and isn't mine.

It's creating my own path with the support of my community.
It's creating my own path with the support of my community.
It's creating my own path with the support of my community.

My healing is being honest about who I am and holding
   myself accountable to my process.
It's feeling my sadness and then going for a long walk to
   figure out next steps.
It's about strengthening my heart so that she and my
   mind can work together in harmony.

My healing is laying my burdens down before God
And wrapping my arms around myself while saying, "It's
   going to be okay."

It's acknowledging that I'm human, have no regrets, and
will learn from the past.

My healing is in truth and reconciliation
And no longer being tied down by the world's
    expectations of me.
It's about reframing old thoughts to set healthy boundaries.

It's in my commune with nature as I greet each living thing.
It's in my commune with nature as I greet each living thing.
It's in my commune with nature as I greet each living thing.

My healing is to be seen with inherent worth, without
    judgement, shame, or guilt.
It's granting myself permission to have self-confidence,
    self-empathy, and self-acceptance.
It's in the hope that things will get better one day, even
    when life is hard.

My healing is movement with light through grief and
    mourning.
It's in the long inhales and exhales of B R E A T H!
My healing is my divine right to dignity.

Based on her story

You in My Reflection

When I look inside myself,
I see your image true.
I open my arms wide
To hold sacred space for you.

I send love to your pain
While I bless your peace.
I welcome you without judgment
And invoke the beauty of your being.

Your shadow is my shadow.
Your light is my light.
Your tears are my tears.
Your fight is my fight.

When I see into myself,
I see your spirit true.
I open my embrace to the sky,
Holding sacred space for you.

Inspired by you